ENSURING SOFTWARE RELIABILITY

QUALITY AND RELIABILITY

A Series Edited by

EDWARD G. SCHILLING
Coordinating Editor
Center for Quality and Applied Statistics
Rochester Institute of Technology
Rochester, New York

W. GROVER BARNARD
Associate Editor for
Human Factors
Vita Mix Corporation
Cleveland, Ohio

RICHARD S. BINGHAM, JR.
Associate Editor for
Quality Management
Consultant
Brooksville, Florida

LARRY RABINOWITZ
Associate Editor for
Statistical Methods
College of William and Mary
Williamsburg, Virginia

THOMAS WITT
Associate Editor for
Statistical Quality Control
Rochester Institute of Technology
Rochester, New York

1. Designing for Minimal Maintenance Expense: The Practical Application of Reliability and Maintainability, *Marvin A. Moss*
2. Quality Control for Profit: Second Edition, Revised and Expanded, *Ronald H. Lester, Norbert L. Enrick, and Harry E. Mottley, Jr.*
3. QCPAC: Statistical Quality Control on the IBM PC, *Steven M. Zimmerman and Leo M. Conrad*
4. Quality by Experimental Design, *Thomas B. Barker*
5. Applications of Quality Control in the Service Industry, *A. C. Rosander*
6. Integrated Product Testing and Evaluating: A Systems Approach to Improve Reliability and Quality, Revised Edition, *Harold L. Gilmore and Herbert C. Schwartz*
7. Quality Management Handbook, *edited by Loren Walsh, Ralph Wurster, and Raymond J. Kimber*

8. Statistical Process Control: A Guide for Implementation, *Roger W. Berger and Thomas Hart*

9. Quality Circles: Selected Readings, *edited by Roger W. Berger and David L. Shores*

10. Quality and Productivity for Bankers and Financial Managers, *William J. Latzko*

11. Poor-Quality Cost, *H. James Harrington*

12. Human Resources Management, *edited by Jill P. Kern, John J. Riley, and Louis N. Jones*

13. The Good and the Bad News About Quality, *Edward M. Schrock and Henry L. Lefevre*

14. Engineering Design for Producibility and Reliability, *John W. Priest*

15. Statistical Process Control in Automated Manufacturing, *J. Bert Keats and Norma Faris Hubele*

16. Automated Inspection and Quality Assurance, *Stanley L. Robinson and Richard K. Miller*

17. Defect Prevention: Use of Simple Statistical Tools, *Victor E. Kane*

18. Defect Prevention: Use of Simple Statistical Tools, Solutions Manual, *Victor E. Kane*

19. Purchasing and Quality, *Max McRobb*

20. Specification Writing and Management, *Max McRobb*

21. Quality Function Deployment: A Practitioner's Approach, *James L. Bossert*

22. The Quality Promise, *Lester Jay Wollschlaeger*

23. Statistical Process Control in Manufacturing, *edited by J. Bert Keats and Douglas C. Montgomery*

24. Total Manufacturing Assurance, *Douglas C. Brauer and John Cesarone*

25. Deming's 14 Points Applied to Services, *A. C. Rosander*

26. Evaluation and Control of Measurements, *John Mandel*

27. Achieving Excellence in Business: A Practical Guide to the Total Quality Transformation Process, *Kenneth E. Ebel*

28. Statistical Methods for the Process Industries, *William H. McNeese and Robert A. Klein*

29. Quality Engineering Handbook, *edited by Thomas Pyzdek and Roger W. Berger*

30. Managing for World-Class Quality: A Primer for Executives and Managers, *Edwin S. Shecter*

31. A Leader's Journey to Quality, *Dana M. Cound*

32. ISO 9000: Preparing for Registration, *James L. Lamprecht*

33. Statistical Problem Solving, *Wendell E. Carr*

34. Quality Control for Profit: Gaining the Competitive Edge. Third Edition, Revised and Expanded, *Ronald H. Lester, Norbert L. Enrick, and Harry E. Mottley, Jr.*

35. Probability and Its Applications for Engineers, *David H. Evans*

36. An Introduction to Quality Control for the Apparel Industry, *Pradip V. Mehta*

37. Total Engineering Quality Management, *Ronald J. Cottman*
38. Ensuring Software Reliability, *Ann Marie Neufelder*
39. Guidelines for Laboratory Quality Auditing, *Donald C. Singer and Ronald P. Upton*

ADDITIONAL VOLUMES IN PREPARATION

Quality by Experimental Design, Second Edition, Revised and Expanded, *Thomas B. Barker*

ENSURING SOFTWARE RELIABILITY

Ann Marie Neufelder
NK Consultants
Hebron, Kentucky

Marcel Dekker, Inc.   New York • Basel • Hong Kong

Library of Congress Cataloging-in-Publication Data

Neufelder, Ann Marie.
    Ensuring software reliability / Ann Marie Neufelder.
      p.   cm.—(Quality and reliability)
    Includes bibliographical references and index.
    ISBN 0-8247-8762-5 (alk. paper)
   1. Computer software—Reliability. I. Title. II. Series
QA76.76.R44N48   1993
005—dc20   92-25561
                                          CIP

This book is printed on acid-free paper.

Marcel Dekker, Inc.
270 Madison Avenue, New York, New York 10016

Current printing (last digit):
10 9 8 7 6 5 4 3 2

To my husband
TOM

About the Series

The genesis of modern methods of quality and reliability will be found in a simple memo dated May 16, 1924, in which Walter A. Shewhart proposed the control chart for the analysis of inspection data. This led to a broadening of the concept of inspection from emphasis on detection and correction of defective material to control of quality through analysis and prevention of quality problems. Subsequent concern for product performance in the hands of the user stimulated development of the systems and techniques of reliability. Emphasis on the consumer as the ultimate judge of quality serves as the catalyst to bring about the integration of the methodology of quality with that of reliability. Thus, the innovations that came out of the control chart spawned a philosophy of control of quality and reliability that has come to include not only the methodology of the statistical sciences and engineering, but also the use of appropriate management methods together with various motivational procedures in a concerted effort dedicated to quality improvement.

This series is intended to provide a vehicle to foster interaction of the elements of the modern approach to quality, including statistical applications, quality and reliability engineering, management, and motivational aspects. It is a forum in which the subject matter of these various areas can be brought together to allow for effective integration of appropriate techniques. This will promote the true benefit of each, which can be achieved only through their interaction. In this sense, the whole of quality and reliability is greater than the sum of its parts, as each element augments the others.

The contributors to this series have been encouraged to discuss fundamental concepts as well as methodology, technology, and procedures at the leading edge of the discipline. Thus, new concepts are placed in proper perspective in these evolving disciplines. The series is intended for those in manufacturing, engineering, and marketing and management, as well as the consuming public, all of whom have an interest and stake in the improvement and maintenance of quality and reliability in the products and services that are the lifeblood of the economic system.

The modern approach to quality and reliability concerns excellence: excellence when the product is designed, excellence when the product is made, excellence as the product is used, and excellence throughout its lifetime. But excellence does not result without effort, and products and services of superior quality and reliability require an appropriate combination of statistical, engineering, management, and motivational effort. This effort can be directed for maximum benefit only in light of timely knowledge of approaches and methods that have been developed and are available in these areas of expertise. Within the volumes of this series, the reader will find the means to create, control, correct, and improve quality and reliability in ways that are cost effective, that enhance productivity, and that create a motivational atmosphere that is harmonious and constructive. It is dedicated to that end and to the readers whose study of quality and reliability will lead to greater understanding of their products, their processes, their workplaces, and themselves.

Edward G. Schilling

Preface

This book is intended for persons from various industries interested in applying software reliability measurement, development, and management concepts in a real environment. Software engineers, reliability engineers, systems engineers, managers, and others interested in the development, measurement, or management of reliable software will find the book useful. It is also suitable for those desiring an overview of software reliability concepts.

The practical versus theoretical aspects of software reliability are concentrated on; however, software reliability theory is presented to some extent in two of the chapters.

Part I lays the foundation for grasping the chapters in Parts II, III, and IV. If you are interested primarily in software reliability measuring, modeling, and predicting, you should read Chapters 2, 3, 6, 7, and 8. If you are interested in designing, coding, testing, or maintaining software for reliability, you should read Chapters 2, 9, 10, 11, and 12. If you are interested in implementing a software reliability program or total quality management, or if you are a software manager, you should as a very minimum read Chapters 1, 2, 5, 6, 7, and 13. If you are interested in system reliability or software reliability allocations, you should read Chapters 1, 4, and 11. Everyone should read Chapter 5.

The book is based on my experience in implementing, developing, and validating software models since 1983. I have worked with every phase of the software life cycle as a software engineer, software reliability engineer, and software manager, and my real-world experiences in measuring, designing, coding, testing, maintaining, improving, and managing software from the perspective of reliability form the content of this book. I have applied these concepts across a broad cross section of products including defense, financial, and engineering software.

Ann Marie Neufelder

Contents

About the Series   *v*
Preface   *vii*

PART I: INRODUCTION TO SOFTWARE
RELIABILITY

1   **Introduction**   **3**

   1.1   Measurement and Analysis of Software   5
          Reliability

   1.2   Development Techniques for Reliable   6
          Software

   1.3   Improving the Process   7

   1.4   Management of the Process   8
          Summary   8

                                          ix

2   Defining Software Reliability   9

   2.1   Software Reliability Definitions   10
   2.2   How Can Software Be Unreliable?   11
   2.3   Why Is Software Reliability Important   13
         Today?
   2.4   The Cost of Unreliable Software   14
         Summary   19
         References   20

3   Software Failures and Failure Processes   21

   3.1   Software Errors, Faults, and Failures   21
   3.2   Software Versus Hardware Failures   30
   3.3   Software Versus Hardware Failure Process   30
         Summary   31
         References   31

4   Government and Industry Objectives   33

   4.1   Measurement of Software Reliability and   34
         Goals for Improving it
   4.2   Allocations for System and Software   40
         Reliability
         Summary   41
         References   42

5   Factors that Affect Software Reliability   45

   5.1   Methodologies and Tools   45
   5.2   Learning Factor   47
   5.3   Organization   48
   5.4   Documentation   48
   5.5   Complexity   50
   5.6   Environment   51
   5.7   Presence of Prototyping   52
   5.8   Requirements Translation and Traceability   54
   5.9   Test Methodology   55
   5.10 Maintenance   57
   5.11 Schedule   57
   5.12 Language   58
   5.13 Existence of Similar Software   58

5.14	Qualitative Characteristics of Software	58
5.15	Tradeoffs of Design Parameters	63
	Summary	63
	References	63

6 Software Reliability Terms and Definitions   **65**

6.1	Types of Software Errors	65
6.2	Criticality of Software Errors	67
6.3	Types of Software Testing	67
6.4	Software Reliability Testing	69
6.5	Randomness of Software Faults	73
6.6	Distribution of Software Faults	74
6.7	Software Reliability Parameters	75
	Summary	77
	References	78

PART II: MEASURING SOFTWARE RELIABILITY

7 Software Reliability Data Collection   **81**

7.1	Collecting and Measuring Error Data Via the Problem-Reporting Process	82
7.2	Process Data to Be Collected	94
7.3	Product Data to Be Collected and Measured	98
7.4	Case Studies	99
	Summary	113
	References	113

8 Software Reliability Models   **125**

8.1	Software Reliability Model Parameters	126
8.2	The Musa Models	127
8.3	Shooman's Model	130
8.4	Jelinski–Moranda Deutrophication Model	132
8.5	Lipow Modified Jelinski–Moranda Model	133
8.6	Goel–Okumoto Model	133
8.7	Jelinski–Moranda Geometric Deutrophication Model	134

8.8	Duane Growth Model	135
8.9	Schick–Wolverton Model	135
8.10	Leone Test Coverage Model	136
8.11	Error Seeding Models	140
8.12	Dual Test Group Model	141
8.13	Testing Success Model	144
8.14	Weibull Model	144
8.15	Predictive Models	146
8.16	Case Studies of Reliability Models	147
	Summary	163
	References	167

PART III: IMPROVING SOFTWARE RELIABILITY

9 Designing for More Reliable Software   171

9.1	Structured Design and Code	171
9.2	Conventions for a Structured Design	173
9.3	Documenting Source Code	175
9.4	Reusability	177
9.5	Fault Tolerance and Error Prevention	179
	Summary	185
	References	192

10 Testing and Maintaining for More Reliable Software   193

10.1	Structural Complexity and Structured Testing	193
10.2	Algorithm Testing	195
10.3	Logical Testing	199
10.4	Maintenance and Regression Testing	200
10.5	Functional Testing	201
	Summary	201
	References	202

11 Software Analyses   203

11.1	Fault-Tree Analysis	204
11.2	Failure Modes Effects and Criticality Analysis	213

| | | Summary | 213 |
| | | References | 214 |

12 Automating Software Reliability **215**

12.1	Tools for Estimating Software Reliability	215
12.2	Analysis Tools	217
12.3	Design Tools	218
12.4	Tools that Compute Complexity	220
12.5	Tools that Produce Test Cases	220
12.6	Configuration Management Tools	221
	Summary	221
	References	222

PART IV: MANAGEMENT OF SOFTWARE RELIABILITY

13 Developing a Program Plan for Software Reliability **225**

13.1	Steps for Implementing Software Reliability at Your Organization	226
13.2	Implementing Software Reliability on a Particular Project	232
13.3	Medium- and Long-Term Objectives	233
13.4	Lessons Learned	236
	Summary	238
	References	238

Index *239*

ENSURING SOFTWARE RELIABILITY

PART I

Introduction to Software Reliability

CHAPTER 1

Introduction

This book addresses four essential areas of software reliability:

1. Measurement and analysis
2. Development techniques for reliable software
3. Improvement of the process
4. Management of the process

Figure 1.1 illustrates the major components of a reliable software development process and therefore the topics that will be addressed by this book.

Originally, in the early and mid-1970s, software engineering principles were researched in order to project scheduling and staffing requirements for software development. Then the focus shifted toward measuring and predicting software fault counts. Recently the emphasis has shifted toward measuring the process and the product as well as the fault counts.

Many articles and books available today concentrate on only one or possibly two of the four topics listed earlier. Each of the four topics de-

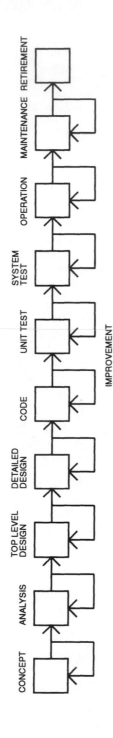

CONCEPT ANALYSIS TOP LEVEL DESIGN DETAILED DESIGN CODE UNIT TEST SYSTEM TEST OPERATION MAINTENANCE RETIREMENT

IMPROVEMENT

SOME MEASUREMENTS, ANALYSES, METHODS OF IMPROVEMENT

PROTOTYPING
LESSONS LEARNED
CUSTOMER INTERFACE
ESTABLISHED PROCESS
RELIABILITY PREDICTION

DESIGN METHODOLOGIES
DESIGN TOOLS
ESTABLISHED DESIGN PROCESS
SOFTWARE DESIGN METRICS
RELIABILITY PREDICTION
FAULT TREE ANALYSIS

CODING STANDARDS
CODE METRICS
RELIABILITY PREDICTION
FAULT TREE ANALYSIS

UNIT TESTING PROCEDURES
SYSTEM TESTING PROCEDURES
TEST COVERAGE METRICS
RELIABILITY ESTIMATION
FAULT TREE ANALYSIS
INDEPENDENT TESTING

MAINTENANCE METHODOLOGIES
MAINTENANCE TOOLS
MAINTENANCE METRICS
VALIDATION OF PREDICTIONS

Figure 1.1 Major components of a software development process.

scribed in this book is dependent on the other three, to a great extent, to be successfully implemented. Measurement and analysis do not serve much of a purpose unless there is an improvement process for which to use those measurements. The software cannot be improved unless there are development techniques for doing so. This whole process cannot be optimized with respect to cost and time without management of the measurement, analysis, improvement, and development methodologies, and the procedures, resources, and schedule. Measurements and analyses are necessary in order to indicate to both management and development the state of the product and the process.

1.1 MEASUREMENT AND ANALYSIS OF SOFTWARE RELIABILITY

The measurement and analysis techniques include software metrics, software reliability models, and software analyses such as fault trees and failure modes effects and criticality (FMECA). Software metrics are measures of some aspect of the software product or process itself. Software reliability models, for the most part, model the failures occurring because of the software. Software analyses enable development personnel to find errors in the software while the software is still in a laboratory environment.

There are many types of software metrics and reliability models. Some of these metrics and models have been shown over time to be invalid. For example, in the 1970s the most commonly used metric was errors per executable source lines of code. Over time, however, it has been found that this metric is not as valuable or valid as originally thought (at least not in many circumstances); see Chapters 4 and 7 for more on this.

Software models and metrics are most useful when used in conjunction with each other and when used during the most appropriate phase or phases of the life cycle. It is not effective to use all existing metrics, nor it is effective to use the incorrect metric. Chapters 7 and 8 discuss which metrics and models to use and when.

It is necessary that metrics and models be used and chosen discriminately. There are some metrics that should be used in every project, such as distribution of error types and total error counts; however, some metrics should only be used if there is reason to believe that the metric will expose some valuable information that will improve the development process. Software reliability models should also be used discriminately because the assumptions of each model vary and may not fit the characteristics of a given software project. A common mistake when implementing some of the reliability models is to adjust the development environment to fit the model instead of finding the model that fits the development environment.

Software analyses will determine some potential sources of error and should be used while designing, coding, and testing the software. Analyses may also be used to prevent critical errors from becoming faults. Software engineers as well as reliability or systems engineers may use these analyses. The results of a fault tree analysis or FMECA will probably be unique to every person who performs it. Some organizations have a software engineer and a systems or reliability engineer perform the analyses so that more than one viewpoint is represented. Chapter 11 discusses these analyses. The author has found that if resources permit, this can be an effective way to detect severe errors before they have manifested themselves in a real environment.

Software measurement and analysis should not necessarily be performed by an independent organization or department. We explore how different metrics, models, and analyses are used by software developers, managers, reliability engineers, systems engineers, and other personnel involved in the process. Software measurement and analysis should not be an isolated part of the process. It must be integrated into the process to be successful.

1.2 DEVELOPMENT TECHNIQUES FOR RELIABLE SOFTWARE

In this book development techniques are techniques used in every phase of the life cycle, from concept to maintenance. The techniques discussed in this book are for the design, code, unit test, integration test, acceptance test, maintenance test, and maintenance phases. These techniques include:

1. Requirements tracing and translation to design and code
2. Design methodologies
3. Code methodologies
4. Unit testing methodologies
5. System testing methodologies
6. Inspections and walkthroughs
7. Error prevention and fault tolerance

Versions of each of these techniques have been shown to be effective in reducing errors and improving maintainability and reliability. Chapters 5, 9, 10, and 11 discuss these.

It has been shown in many studies that modular, structured design and code are less prone to errors than code that is not modular or structured. The design, code, unit test, system test, and maintenance techniques discussed are based on these principles. There exist methods of unit testing and system testing that most effectively cover the most source code and the most functionality. There are also methods for performing more effective walkthroughs and inspections in order to detect errors before they occur. Many of the more costly errors are those that may be found by inspection before they become costly. Fault tolerance may be achieved at various levels depending on the software being developed. All software may be fault tolerant with respect to error and input/output (I/O) checking. Some mission-critical software or systems may require redundancy to achieve the required level of system availability.

1.3 IMPROVING THE PROCESS

The improvement process is the feedback from measurement to development. It depends on using the right metrics at the right time and being able to interpret the results of those metrics in a timely enough fashion to impact the end product. It is an ongoing process that never ends. The improvement depends on:

1. Ability to implement the correct measurements and correctly interpret outputs of that measurement.
2. Efficiency of the measurements used; ability to produce results in a practical amount of time with practical amounts of resources.
3. Interface between individuals and groups responsible for developing, measuring, analyzing, and managing the software. A clear definition of tasks is required to develop and improve the software.
4. Ability to make necessary changes to the development process and respond to the results of the measurements within a practical and reasonable time period in order to improve the software.
5. Ability to continue to repeat steps 1 through 4. The cycle does not end. It can and should be continued from one project to the next.

1.4   MANAGEMENT OF THE PROCESS

Management is performing tradeoffs of software design parameters including reliability, scheduling personnel effectively, and implementing procedures for measurement, development, and improvement. There are some software metrics that were intended to aid management decisions. Some of these management indicators are the estimated projected number of errors to exist after some period of time, the estimated cost of each corrective action, the estimated time required to detect some number of errors, and the average turnaround time for error corrections.

SUMMARY

Development of reliable software is dependent on each of the following:

1. Correct selection and usage of metrics, models, and analyses
2. Correct interpretation of the results of metrics, models, and analyses
3. Feedback from measurement and analysis results to the development process in a practical period of time
4. Response to measurement results to improve the development process
5. Development techniques and methodologies that optimize reliability and maintainability as well as other design parameters or quality factors
6. Interfacing between personnel to perform the required tasks necessary to measure, analyze, develop, and improve the software with respect to reliability
7. Implementation of the necessary procedures for accomplishing these tasks
8. Scheduling of personnel and resources to optimize for the necessary design parameters, including reliability
9. Keeping the measurement and analysis, development, improvement, and management process going

We will see in each of the following chapters how to measure, analyze, develop, improve, and manage for reliable software.

CHAPTER 2

Defining Software Reliability

What is software reliability? Software reliability is a relatively new concept, and although industry and government have been making efforts to standardize it, to date, no one definition of software reliability nor one method of measuring or predicting software reliability is accepted as standard. There are many models and metrics available today for estimating software reliability and measuring characteristics of software. Some of these models have been invalidated, some are currently being validated, and some have been shown to be valid during some phases of the life cycle but not others. The question remaining today is whether or not it is possible for one model to be standardized for all applications, or whether a combination of models is appropriate. There is also a question of whether or not it is feasible to predict the reliability of software before it is even developed.

This chapter addresses the definition of software reliability, how software can be unreliable, why software reliability is important today, and the cost of unreliable software.

2.1   SOFTWARE RELIABILITY DEFINITIONS

Some of the most commonly accepted definitions of software reliability
follow.

The Institute of Electrical and Electronic Engineers (IEEE) defines
software reliability as

> the probability that software will not cause a system failure for a specified
> time under specified conditions. The probability is a function of the inputs
> to, and use of, the system as well as function of the existence of faults in
> the software. The inputs to the system determine whether existing faults,
> if any, are encountered.

John Musa of AT&T Bell Laboratories defines software reliability as

> the probability that a given software system operates for some time period
> without software error, on the machine for which it was designed, given
> that it is used within design limits.

Dr. Martin Shooman of the New York Polytechnical University defines software reliability as

> the probability of failure free operation of a computer program for a spec-
> ified time in a specified environment.

This definition is similar to the definition for hardware reliability.

The following is the author's definition of reliable software as opposed
to a definition of software reliability.

> Reliable software is a function of (1) ability to meet requirements, (2) abil-
> ity to perform under a variety of inputs and environments (assuming they
> are in range of the requirements), (3) ability for faults to be maintained,
> (4) ability for the software to be tested and verified, (5) ability for the
> software to continue functioning once a fault has been encountered.

I define reliable software as opposed to software reliability in order to
make objective those characteristics of software that determine how reliable the software will be.

From a broad perspective, software reliability may be defined in a
similar manner to hardware reliability. The Musa and Shooman definitions closely resemble the definition of reliable hardware. The one aspect

of software reliability that is missing from these definitions is the ability for the software to meet the requirements. This may appear to be trivial; however, statistics from a variety of sources confirm that the requirements definition has a major impact on the reliability of software. This is discussed in detail in Chapter 3.

The Musa, Shooman, and IEEE definitions also do not define what exactly a software failure is. When defining software reliability it is important also to define what a software failure is, due to the fact that a software failure may be confused with a hardware failure due to aging, fatigue, etc. Software does fail, but does not fail for the same reasons that hardware fails; see Chapter 3 for more on software failures.

2.2 HOW CAN SOFTWARE BE UNRELIABLE?

The following are some examples of unreliable medical, financial, defense, space, air traffic control, transportation, and communication software:

- Interest due on very large loan amounts is not accurate because of loss of precision in financial software.
- Interest accumulated on very large deposits is not accurate because of loss of precision in financial software.
- Bills for negative amounts are sent because of inflexible software.
- Bills are sent with incorrect amounts, or bills are sent to the wrong person, because of incorrect data and/or calculations.
- Reservations are canceled erroneously because of incorrect data or algorithms.
- Incorrect airline or hotel reservations are made because of incorrect data or algorithms.
- Incorrect checking account balances are due to incorrect calculation of debits, credits, fees, or incorrect teller software.
- Electronic warfare systems fail to identify a real threat.
- Electronic warfare systems identify a threat when there is none.
- Aircraft failure is identified improperly or not at all.
- Aircraft failure is identified when there is none.
- Incorrect doses are prescribed to a patient due to incorrect medical software.
- Patients receive the wrong medicine due to incorrect medical software.

- Customer databases or any other database loses data when a system limit such as 32768 is reached.
- Loss of telephone communication due to a software error.
- Denial of credit due to software error.
- Loss of business data or client data due to a maximum number of entries reached in software logic.
- Loss of business data due to erroneous file management procedures in software.

The precise reasons for unreliable software may be one or more of the following:

- Data not organized correctly or efficiently.
- User inputs not extensive enough.
- The variables that define the amounts may be floating point as opposed to double floating point.
- Integer values are used where there should be floating points.
- Integers are not defined to be large enough for the possible number of entries which may be stored.
- Software functions are not complete or do not perform the correct function.
- Response times are not adequate due to I/O and memory resources not being optimized.
- Not enough or any error checking on status and I/O.
- Too much error checking on status and I/O.
- Assignment of global variables performed incorrectly.
- Incorrect parameter passing.
- Read and/or write errors.
- Algorithm errors due to numbers that become too large or too small (divide by zero, square root of a negative number, multiplication of two very large numbers or two very small numbers, etc.).
- Indexes of arrays that become out of range.
- Lack of initialization of variables.
- Erroneous initialization of variables.
- A software requirement overlooked or defined incorrectly.
- An algorithm incorrectly coded (i.e., parenthesis in the wrong location).
- Incorrect flow of logic.
- Incorrect file handling.
- Installation procedures not complete or correct.

- Multipoint error due to a combination of events.
- Error trapping on user inputs too restrictive or not restrictive enough.

There are many other types of errors that will cause software to become unreliable. The ones just listed are some of the most common ones. Software can also be unreliable when it does not perform the function that the end user intended or required. There are also deficiencies in software that affect the user interface. Some examples of user interface errors or user-unfriendly errors are:

- Information is not organized properly or as expected by the user.
- Instructions are unclear, inconsistent, or missing.
- Correct user responses are unclear or misleading.
- User is not informed when an error has occurred.
- User's documentation is not consistent with the software, or is incorrect, ambiguous, or incomplete.

2.3 WHY IS SOFTWARE RELIABILITY IMPORTANT TODAY?

There are at least four major reasons why reliable software has become a very important issue in the last decade or so.

1. Systems are becoming software intensive. Many flight systems are becoming more software intensive than hardware intensive. Financial systems including teller, automated teller, and loan processing are software intensive. Defense and energy systems are becoming more software intensive. Everything from insurance rates to credit histories to hotel reservations to long-distance telephone calls is performed by software. Software affects our daily lives.

2. Many software-intensive systems are safety critical. Flight systems, electronic warfare systems, radar, air traffic control, medical systems, energy systems, and space systems are all software-intensive systems that are also safety critical. Even systems that are not safety critical may be mission critical, meaning that success is critical to some end purpose (such as defeating an enemy at war), or failure is extremely costly financially.

3. Customers are requiring more reliable software. Many govern-

ment contracts are now requiring that an established level of software reliability be achieved. Software has also become part of the system reliability allocations on many government contracts. Commercial clients are also requiring more reliable systems, and many are attempting to establish the same criteria as the government for development of reliable software. At one time, software reliability was assumed to be 1 for purposes of determining system reliability. Those days are behind us.

Software errors similar to the ones described in the previous section are not being tolerated by end users or by clients of end users. Financial institutions, medical institutions, the government, communication corporations, and other corporations are in a position of being legally liable for software that is not accurate, that causes potential loss of life or loss of mission, that causes inconvenience to end users, and that causes end users to lose profits. In addition to being liable, users and developers of software are also facing increasing maintenance costs.

4.   The cost of developing software is increasing. Data from a variety of sources show that for many systems developing the software is becoming one of the major costs of the system, if not *the* major cost. Much of the software cost can be associated with corrective action, particularly corrective action late in the development cycle. The cost of maintaining software has been shown in some studies to be as much as 40–70% of the total development cost. Some NASA and Air Force sources have estimated it to be 50% of their development cost.

2.4   THE COST OF UNRELIABLE SOFTWARE

The cost of correcting a software error generally increases by magnitudes for every phase of the life cycle. Figure 2.1 represents the number of errors that are detected over time starting from unit test to field usage. Ideally, most of the errors are detected by the end of the unit testing phase. This can be associated with the burn-in phase for hardware. The other curves in this figure represent the event that errors are not found early during unit testing. The author has represented data from many software programs with a graph similar to that in Figure 2.1 and has witnessed all of the three types of curves. The curve representing the "'usually disaster" most often occurred due to continually changing requirements, new requirements made after the design and/or code was complete, and design errors.

Ideally, the errors found during the integration phase are those due to

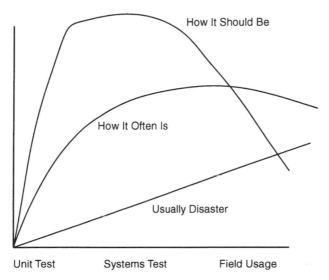

How It Should Be

How It Often Is

Usually Disaster

Unit Test   Systems Test   Field Usage

Figure 2.1   Number of errors detected over life cycle.

interfaces that could not have been easily or possibly found during previous phases. Ideally the number of errors detected levels off by the acceptance test phase.

If it is known what the average cost of fixing a bug is during each phase of the life cycle, it can be estimated what the cost of repair is and also what it could be. If the average cost is not known, then the relative cost may be found by comparing real errors detected over time against the ideal.

If a curve such as this one is to be used as a software metric for improvement, it should not be used alone. Additional data must be collected to determine the types and causes of these errors. For example, if you plotted errors over life cycle and discovered that most of your errors were found during integration and acceptance testing, your first reaction might be that you are not performing sufficient unit testing. However, it is entirely possible that the types of errors detected were due to changes in requirements or additional requirements due to insufficient requirements translations, as opposed to insufficient unit testing. By collecting additional information on the error types you would have a basis for making improvements in your software development process.

Figure 2.2 represents real cost data collected on a cross section of pro-

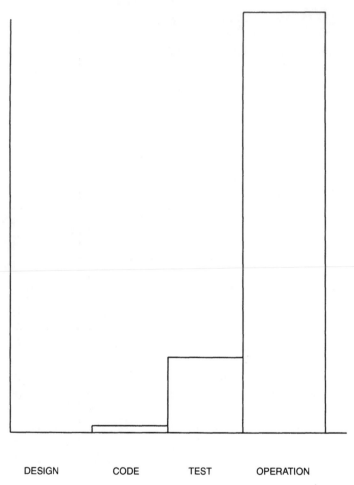

DESIGN   CODE   TEST   OPERATION

Figure 2.2   Minimum cost of correcting a software error.

grams, indicating that the cost of fixing a software error multiplied by
more than 10 for every phase of the life cycle (the multiplier was approximately 14). This cost includes the cost of manpower, travel ex-
penses, cost of losing a customer, etc.

The following government data concern the cost of reliable software.
Even though these figures pertain to certain types of software delivered
to the government, they may be applied to commercial software due to

the large cross section of data collected by the government as shown next.

Problems encountered by the government in delivered software include:

1. Errors detected after delivery
2. Requirements not translated correctly
3. Product not complete
4. Difficulty in supporting software
5. Apparent lack of a systematic process

These problems were encountered for fighter/attack systems, avionics, electronic warfare (EW), navigation, radar, and ground-based systems. Some of these types of problems can and do represent any type of software development regardless of its application type. Number 5 seems to summarize the source for numbers 1 through 4. The lack of a systematic process is evident at a cross section of software development organizations. A systematic process includes more than just adhering to software standards such as Mil-Hdbk 2167A. A systematic process is one that begins at the concept phase and ends at retirement. It includes measurement and improvement of the software. See Chapter 13 for more information on a systematic process.

The distribution of errors in the life cycle phases was:

1. Requirements and design, 64%
2. Coding, 36%

The author has found similar results on a cross section of software applications including military, engineering, insurance, and finance software, with 70% due to requirements and design and 30% due to coding. We can see in the programs used for these studies that most of the errors were introduced before the code was even developed. In order to determine how costly these errors are, we must also know when these errors were detected and, using the cost data in Figure 2.2, determine approximately how much the maintenance is costing us.

The following is the distribution of errors by phase in which they were encountered:

1. Requirements, 9%
2. Design, 2%

3. Code, 7%
4. Software integration, 15%
5. Systems integration, 48%
6. Flight test, 13%
7. Operation, 6%

We can see by these data that almost half of the errors are found while the software is being integrated into the system. Another study by Hewlett-Packard found that an average of 50% of all of the development effort was spent during the maintenance phase. If we assume that the cost of fixing an error is multiplied by 10 for every phase just listed, then we can see what our cost benefit would be if we found some percentage of errors earlier in the life cycle.

Out of the total number of errors, the types of errors were distributed as follows:

1. Documentation, 2%
2. Computation, 5%
3. Human, 5%
4. Environment, 5%
5. Interface, 6%
6. Data, 6%
7. Other, 7%
8. Logic, 28%
9. Requirements translation, 36%

The author has found similar results:

1. Logic (design and code), 38%
2. Requirements translation, 32%
3. The other 29% varied tremendously from program to program

The author has found that though the proportion of logic/code and requirements errors remained somewhat constant from program to program, the other types of errors varied depending on the application. These results should not discourage you from measuring these percentages at your own organization. These results are shown as a ballpark estate of what you might expect at your own company.

The preceding data were collected on four completely different types of software applications: financial, insurance, engineering, and military.

Chapter 7 contains a breakdown of this data by these types of applications.

According to another set of government data the cost of these software problems to the government is:

1. Software cost overruns of 20–30% and sometimes even 1000%.
2. Sixty percent of the errors were made during the requirements phase but only about 15% of the errors were caught in that phase. This compares closely to the previous set of government data, which showed 64% of all errors were made during the requirements phase but only 9% were detected during that phase.
3. Systems are delivered with 3 errors per 1000 lines of executable source code.

The author has found that estimating errors per lines of code is misleading due to the fact that languages vary and the fact that efficient programmers may write fewer lines of code than less efficient programmers. However, in one case, the author experienced a situation where the language used was always PASCAL and programmer efficiency was relatively constant due to the fact that all of the programmers had nearly the same educational background and years of experience. In that case the errors per lines of code was counted for various software projects and it was found that the average was 7 errors per 1000 lines of code at the point in time when the software was delivered. The interesting note in this case was that the stated requirement for errors per lines of code was also 7 per 1000.

SUMMARY

On a variety of programs developed for various industries and the government it has been shown that most of the software errors were introduced early in the development cycle, yet most of them were not found until the integration testing phase and later. Data collected by various researchers have shown that the cost of correcting a software error increases for every phase of the life cycle by some magnitude. The cost benefit of detecting and correcting errors early in the life cycle can be shown by multiplying the number of errors found in each phase of the life cycle by the appropriate magnitude (if it is unknown, make an assumption).

REFERENCES

Air Force Systems Command. *Software Quality Insight*, AFSCP 800-14. January 1987.

Babel, Phil. *Software Development Integrity Program*. Aeronautical Systems Division, Wright Patterson Air Force Base, OH, 1988.

Beizer, Boris. *Software Systems Testing & Quality Assurance*. Van Nostrand Reinhold, New York, 1984.

Dinitto, Samuel. *Project Forecast II Software Quality & Productivity*. IEEE Publications, RAMS Proceedings, Philadelphia, PA, 1987.

Grady, R., and Caswell, D. *Software Metrics: Establishing a Company Wide Program*. Hewlett-Packard Company, Prentice-Hall, Englewood Cliffs, NJ, 1987.

IEEE Guide for the Use of IEEE Standard Dictionary of Measures to Produce Reliable Software, IEEE Standard 982.2. IEEE Publications, New York, 1988.

IEEE Standard Dictionary of Measures to Produce Reliable Software, IEEE Standard 982.1. 1988, IEEE Publications, New York, 1988.

Koss, W. Edward. *Software Reliability Metrics for Military Systems*. IEEE Publications, RAMS Proceedings, Los Angeles, 1988.

Musa, J., Iannino, A., and Okumuto, K. *Software Reliability Measurement, Prediction, Application*. McGraw-Hill, New York, 1987.

Proceedings of the Eleventh Annual Software Engineering Workshop, SEL-86-006, Greenbelt, MD, December 1986.

RADC-TR-87-171 Methodology for Software Prediction. Air Force Systems Command, Griffiss Air Force Base, New York, 1987.

Shooman, Martin. *Software Engineering: Design, Reliability, and Management*. McGraw-Hill, New York, 1987.

CHAPTER 3

Software Failures and Failure Processes

In some ways software reliability may be modeled, designed for, improved, and managed in a similar manner to hardware, but in many other ways it may not. This chapter identifies the similarities and differences between hardware and software reliability. Software error, fault, and failure are also defined in this chapter. It is very important to understand exactly what a software failure is before reading the other chapters and even before comparing software reliability to hardware reliability.

3.1 SOFTWARE ERRORS, FAULTS, AND FAILURES

Software errors are the human design errors made either by misinterpretation of requirements or by design or code errors. These errors may or may not be observed or detected by the end user. In practical terms, the total number of errors is unknown and thus estimated since it may never be known, in complete certainty, if every error has been discovered. A detected error is an error that is observed and known. A corrected error is a detected error that has been fixed.

Software faults are the manifestation of a software error. This is an error that is now detected by the user in some form. The user may not know, and probably will not know, the source of the error. A fault is always an error, but an error may or may not be a fault.

Software failures are software faults that cause a system failure. Some software faults may be software failures, but all software failures are software faults and thus software errors. Corrected errors are those errors that have been fixed but may or may not be integrated into the current versions of software. Verified corrected errors are those errors that have been fixed and are verified to exist in the most current release of the software. See the illustration in Figure 3.1.

One very big issue today is determining whether a software anomaly is really an error or an enhancement. An enhancement is a suggestion for a change to the software that may greatly improve its marketability

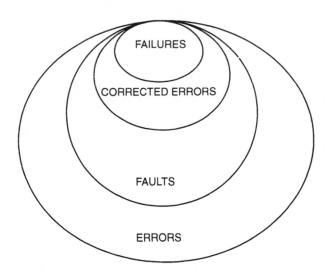

NUMBER OF ERRORS CAN ONLY BE ESTIMATED
NUMBER OF CORRECTED ERRORS <= NUMBER OF ERRORS
NUMBER OF FAULTS <= NUMBER OF ERRORS
NUMBER OF FAILURES <= NUMBER OF ERRORS

Figure 3.1   Software errors, corrected errors, faults, and failures.

but does not have to be made under the realm of the present requirements definition and is not required either contractually or ethically.
What exactly determines whether an anomaly is really an error that
must be fixed, or an enhancement that may or may not have to be
made? Enhancements may not always be obvious as such. For example,
there may be software that functions properly on some number of different platforms, but does not function properly on one particular platform. Is the anomaly when the software does not function on some particular platform an error? A fault? A failure? The author has found that
asking two simple questions may supply the answer. Do the requirements specify that the software function on that platform (or in this
manner)? And does it *have* to be fixed? If the answer to either question
is yes, then more than likely it is because it is an error (now a fault or
failure) that must be fixed.

If you are developing software under a fixed-price contract, this issue
will probably be an important one for you. If you are not working under
a fixed-priced contract, you will probably still need to know where to
draw the line between what must be fixed in order to satisfy the customer's requirements, and what may be fixed to satisfy a customer's expec-
tations. It must be determined which anomalies are errors and which
anomalies are enhancements in order to estimate software reliability accurately.

Classifying *all* anomalies as software errors and fixing them all will
probably not be cost-effective, although there are some development organizations that employ this philosophy. Unfortunately, you could be
giving customers a Cadillac when they have paid for a Volkswagen.
However, if you determine that a software error is completely driven by
a written set of requirements, then you may not be securing future business. There are some requirements that cannot be explicitly stated in a
finite amount of space or time. Therefore, it is probable that some customer requirements will not be explicitly stated. A developer that cannot
recognize that some of these implicit requirements must be addressed
may not remain competitive.

It is generally agreed that anomalies that are in direct conflict with
contractual requirements are indeed an error and must be fixed. However, how should implicit requirements or unstated requirements be
handled? Table 3.1 is a matrix that classifies many anomalies that may
be detected, first as either an error or an enhancement, and according to
how critical the error or enhancement is. As seen in the matrix, in many
cases more than one criticality type is checked. This indicates that de-

Table 3.1   Matrix of Software Anomalies[a]

Description	Error			Enhancement		
	C	M	N	C	M	N
Anomaly is detected in a function that is explicitly required.						
Required function is missing.	x	x				
Required function is present but incorrect:						
causes incorrect outputs	x	x	x			
causes loss of data	x	x				
causes data corruption	x					
error causes incorrect data	x	x	x			
causes a crash	x					
causes annoying outputs		x	x			
causes a hangup	x	x				
Required function causes the user to make an error that:						
is annoying but has no effect on the system functionality			x			
causes incorrect outputs	x	x	x			
causes loss of data	x	x				
causes data corruption	x					
causes incorrect data	x	x				
causes a crash	x	x				
causes annoying outputs		x	x			
causes a hangup	x	x				
Required function is not easy to use by end user:						
is annoying but has no effect on system			x			
requires knowledge of user that the average end user does not have and never will have	x	x				
Anomaly due to ambiguous requirements stated by the customer:						
Could have been avoided by						

Table 3.1 (Continued)

Description	Error			Enhancement		
	C	M	N	C	M	N
developer via inspection of requirements, code, walkthroughs, etc.	x	x	x			
Error in requirements specification could not have been easily identified by the development team				x	x	x
Anomaly is detected in a function that is not explicitly required by end user and was not developed:						
Function was never agreed upon by customer and developer and is not crucial to the ability for the system to function.						x
Function was never agreed upon by customer and developer and is not crucial to ability for system to function; however, the existence of the feature would greatly improve the product and its potential				x	x	
Function was never explicitly stated but was implicitly required due to:						
prevent incorrect outputs	x	x	x			
prevent loss of data	x	x				
prevent data corruption	x					
prevent incorrect data	x	x	x			
prevent a crash	x	x				
prevent annoying outputs			x			
prevent a hangup	x	x				
Anomaly is detected that is not explicitly prohibited by						

Table 3.1 (Continued)

Description	Error			Enhancement		
	C	M	N	C	M	N
requirements:						
causes incorrect outputs	X	X	X			
causes loss of data	X	X				
causes data corruption	X					
causes incorrect data	X	X	X			
causes a crash	X	X				
causes annoying outputs			X			
causes a hangup	X	X				
is a minor nuisance to						
the end user			X			
is a nuisance to the						
end user's clients (if any)				X	X	
Anomaly is detected in a function						
that is not explicitly or implicitly						
required but was developed and						
delivered anyway:						
causes incorrect outputs	X	X	X			
causes loss of data	X	X				
causes data corruption	X					
causes incorrect data	X	X	X			
causes a crash	X	X				
causes annoying outputs			X			
causes a hangup	X	X				
causes the user to make an error						
that:						
is annoying but has no effect						
on the system functionality			X			
causes incorrect outputs	X	X	X			
causes loss of data	X	X				
causes data corruption	X					
causes incorrect data	X	X	X			
causes a crash	X	X				
causes annoying outputs			X			
causes a hangup	X	X				

Table 3.1   (Continued)

Description	Error			Enhancement		
	C	M	N	C	M	N
Required function is not easy to use by end user: is annoying but has no effect on system			X			

*Key: C, critical anomaly; M, moderate anomaly; N, negligible anomaly.

pending on the extent of the damage, the type of error may be of more than one criticality. Critical errors are those that have no work-around and cause loss of function or mission. Moderate errors are those which have a work-around but still have potential for loss of function or mission. Negligible errors are those that do not affect to any great extent the functionality of the system (see the criticality of errors description in Chapter 6).

This matrix is best used as a guideline for establishing company or project-specific guidelines for determining which anomalies are really errors and which are not. Depending on the company, the project, and the end user, the exact implementation of an anomaly classification scheme will vary. Some organizations develop software that must be extremely marketable (i.e., user-friendly) in order to keep the company in business; therefore, all anomalies are considered to be errors and must be corrected. Those companies would need to model all anomalies when estimating software reliability. Other organizations develop software that is developed for one specific end user with one fixed price. Those organizations may not find it cost-effective or even possible to consider every anomaly to be an error that must be corrected.

The first section of errors described are errors that are detected in some function that is explicitly (contractually) required to function. These types of errors include:

1. Required function(s) that are missing
2. A required function not implemented correctly
3. A required function that causes the user to make an error

4. A required function that is not easy to use by the intended end user
5. A required function that does not function properly as the user viewed the requirements, but does function properly as the developer viewed the requirements

Except for one special case, any anomaly in this section is some type of error as opposed to an enhancement. If an error is due to ambiguous requirements but that error could have been avoided by the development team during walkthroughs, inspections, etc., then the error is a error; otherwise it may be an enhancement, since the end user did not clearly state the requirements.

Another section of errors deals with those functions not explicitly required by the requirements. These types of errors are those that:

1. Are due to features that do not exist, that were never stated by the requirements, and are not necessary for functionality.
2. Are due to features that do not exist, that were never stated by the requirements, but would greatly improve the software.
3. Are due to features that do not exist, that were implicitly required to prevent a variety of unexpected results.
4. Are not explicitly prohibited by the requirements but cause a variety of unexpected results. Anomalies of this type are a mixture of errors and enhancements. The general rule of thumb with this section of errors is that if the anomaly results in a loss of data, corruption of data or some other critical result, then the anomaly is an error and must be fixed regardless of what the requirements state.

The third section of anomalies are those found in a function that was not an explicitly required function but that was developed by the developer anyway. Basically, these are anomalies found in code that was a delivered but not required by the requirements (freebie). The rationale for determining the difference between a failure and an enhancement is that even if the customer did not specify the feature, if an organization develops it and gives it to the customer, that organization will be responsible for maintaining it.

Listed next are real examples of each of the errors just described. In many of these cases it was not immediately obvious whether each of the anomalies detected was really a failure or whether it was an improvement or enhancement. In many cases the criticality was not immediately obvious either.

1.   A database was developed for a small business person with no computer experience. During the requirements phase the client was asked how many clients he had. The question was asked in order to determine the best approach to optimizing the computer resources; however, the client did not realize this. The client responded that he had 250–300 clients. The client was asked if that was expected to change at any time in the next few years. The client responded that it was not. The database was developed to efficiently handle 500 clients. Six months later, the client complained that the software was excruciating slow to use. The slowness was costing him time and therefore money. It was found that 650 client records had been entered. The client insisted that the software be changed to handle any number of client records. His argument was that at the time he purchased the software he did have 250 clients; however, his business grew. The developers argument was that the initial requirements were more than exceeded. This problem was eventually determined to be an enhancement due to the fact that the requirements were met and exceeded. However, the developer negotiated the price of the enhancement in order to keep the client. This is also an example of software that met the requirements but was inflexible to change or enhancement.

2.   An organization developed a product such that when a certain combination of keystrokes were executed, some user data was deleted without warning. The organization chose to document this anomaly in the user manual and warned against using this keystroke combination. Is this an error? Even though the failure is warned against in the manual, the user is not explicitly warned by the software, and the failure does cause a loss of data. In this case the anomaly is an error and not an enhancement.

3.   An organization developed software that had one capability to perform a backup and restore of data. If a floppy disk was used for the backup and it was completely full during the backup, the software terminated the backup. Unfortunately, the user was not notified that the backup was terminated and assumed that the backup was successful. Later the user would discover this, long after deleting the data. In this case, the user actually deleted his or her own data; however, it was due to misleading software. This was determined to be an error due to the loss of data and the fact that it *had* to be corrected.

3.2   SOFTWARE VERSUS HARDWARE
FAILURES

Hardware failures, on the other hand, are hardware faults that cause a system failure. System failures may be classified as software or hardware or other (such as user). The mechanism for a hardware failure versus a software failure is not the same; however, both hardware and software failures have the effect of a degradation of the system. Hardware fails due to physical stress, time, wearing out, the elements such as wind, rain, snow, and temperature, and other environmental factors.

Software fails as shown previously by human design error during requirements, design, code, test, or maintenance of the software. In the author's experiences as a teacher of software reliability, one common assumption is, "Software doesn't break." If you view software failures from a hardware perspective, then of course software does not fail. However, if you view software failures from a software perspective, then you will see that software may exhibit the same life-cycle bathtub curve as hardware, only for different reasons.

Software *may* exhibit a burn-in phase in which the reliability of the software steadily increases due to debugging, testing, and error correction. At some point the reliability of the software will probably remain relatively constant while in operation. The author has seen more than one occasion where the software did not do either of these because of continual changes in the requirements long after coding of the software had begun. In those circumstances the software was scrapped and rewritten or abandoned.

Software may or may not exhibit the last phase of the bathtub curve. Assuming that there are no additions or changes made to the software other than purely maintenance changes, eventually the software may exhibit wearout or an increasing failure rate. The increasing failure rate in this case is not due to anything other than error introduction due to maintenance. Over time the documentation necessary for proper repair of software may be lost or not maintained until the point where the error correction process is introducing more errors than eliminating. This will happen if the software is not modular, testable, or maintainable.

3.3   SOFTWARE VERSUS HARDWARE
FAILURE PROCESS

There is some confusion today as to whether or not software reliability is probabilistic (the software reliability can be stated in terms of some fraction between 0.0 and 1.0) or deterministic (0 or 1). A deterministic approach is that the software either is reliable or is not—there is no in between. Depending on how your are viewing software reliability, either statement can be true. If you are viewing the reliability of the software from a very low level, possibly at the executable line-of-code level, then it seems that software reliability is deterministic. Either the instruction will execute properly or it will not. However, if you view software reliability from a much larger perspective, say, one or more entire hardware/software systems in field usage, then it may appear that software reliability is probabilistic, since over time there is some likelihood of a system failure occurring and since it will never be known with complete confidence that the software is completely error free.

One interesting note on the subject of deterministic and probabilistic reliability is that the author has found that the severity assigned to almost all errors ever tracked on a cross section of projects, industries, and companies have been classified by the end user predominantly as either critical or noncritical, as opposed to some range of criticality (i.e., 1 through 3 or 1 through 5, with 1 being most critical). This indicates that end users may view software errors deterministically as either those that they can live with or those that they cannot.

SUMMARY

Chapter 3 discussed:

1. The definition of software errors, faults, failures, corrected errors, and verified corrected errors.
2. The difference between a software error, which must be fixed contractually, legally, or ethically, and an enhancement, which does not have to be implemented but may be to remain competitive.
3. The comparison of software reliability to hardware. Software may exhibit the same life-cycle bathtub curve as hardware.
4. The differences as well as similarities in the software and hardware failure processes.

REFERENCE

IEEE Standard Glossary of Software Engineering Terminology, ANSII-IEEE Standard 729. IEEE Publications, New York, 1983.

CHAPTER 4

Government and Industry Objectives

The government as well as industry have been making attempts to standardize software reliability. The areas that are currently being addressed are:

1. Measuring software reliability
2. Developing methods for improving software reliability
3. Developing system allocations for software reliability

There are some standards, guidelines, and technical reports available today; however, there does not exist at this writing one standard that is commonly accepted for measuring software reliability. This chapter addresses what has been developed to date by both the government and industry.

4.1 MEASUREMENT OF SOFTWARE RELIABILITY AND GOALS FOR IMPROVING IT

The Institute for Electrical and Electronic Engineers (IEEE) has published a Standard Dictionary of Measures to Produce Reliable Software and a Guide for the Use of IEEE Standard Dictionary of Measures to Produce Reliable Software, numbered IEEE Standards 982.1 and 982.2.

These guidelines describe product metrics that are measures of errors, failure rate, reliability growth, remaining faults, completeness, complexity, and so on.

Process metrics are also included that measure management, risks, benefits, costs, and other process variables. The guidelines contain 39 process and product metrics and some guidelines for using these metrics.

Some of the metrics discussed in the IEEE standards are also contained in the Software Quality Indicators Pamphlet (AFSCP 800-14) produced by the Department of the Air Force. One of the metrics contained in both documents is the design structure metric. The metric is intended to find problems with a design. It is based on:

1. The percentage of modules dependent on input or output
2. The percentage of modules dependent on prior processing
3. The percentage of database elements that are not unique
4. Number of database segments per database elements
5. Percentage of modules that have one entrance and exit
6. Whether or not the software was designed from the top down (0 or 1)

These primitives are considered to influence the following design factors, which when summed will equal some number between 0 and 1:

1. Module dependence
2. Module dependence on prior processing
3. Database size
4. Database compartmentalization
5. Modularity with respect to one entrance and exit
6. Structuredness

A good result using this metric is closest to zero. Each of these six design factors may also be weighted for importance. The author uses this metric in its converse to yield an optimum result near 1 and found it extremely useful for evaluating a project design.

The Software Quality Indicators Pamphlet also includes a design completeness metric. This metric is based on:

1. Percentage of functions defined correctly
2. Percentage of data references that have an origin
3. Percentage of defined functions that are used
4. Percentage of all decision points that do not use all conditions
5. Percentage of defined referenced functions
6. Percentage of decision-point conditions with processing
7. Percentage of calling routine parameters with matching defined parameters to the called routine.
8. Percentage of all decision-point conditions that are set
9. Percentage of all set decision-point conditions that have processing
10. Percentage of data references that have a destination

Each of the design factors is summed and can be weighted to yield a result between 0 and 1. According to the Air Force document, a result of 0.73 is the minimum acceptable for design completeness and 0.60 is the minimum acceptable for design structure. These metrics are intended to be used over time to monitor improvement until the acceptable level is achieved or surpassed.

Another software reliability measure discussed by both the IEEE and Air Force documents is the defect density. This is the cumulative errors found during design and code inspections divided by the total number of software units or modules. The metric is intended to be used early in the life cycle from requirements analysis to code and to be updated on a regular and periodic basis based on results of inspections that should also be regular and periodic.

The metric is intended to aid in detection of errors earlier in the life cycle. The author had found this metric to be extremely valuable because it can be used early in the life cycle and because it is based on the modules of code as opposed to the executable line of code.

If a module of code represents one complete function, this metric may be used to compare projects developed in different languages. If defects per lines of code is used instead, there is the risk that all lines of code are not equal from language to language and from function to function. An experienced coder will probably utilize fewer lines of code than an inexperienced one to perform the same function. Some languages are also more dense than others (requiring more lines of code to perform the same function).

The Air Force Pamphlet indicates that 55% of all life-cycle errors are estimated to be introduced in the analysis phase, 30% during design, 10% during code and test, and 5% during maintenance. However, according to the pamphlet, only 18% are found during the analysis phase, 10% during design, 59% during code and test, and 22% while in operation. The Air Force Pamphlet is designed to aid developers in detecting software errors earlier in the life cycle.

The IEEE documents and the Software Quality Indicators both stress improvement via the use of process and product metrics. Software reliability prediction, however, is not directly discussed in either source.

The Air Force's Rome Air Development Center (RADC) has produced a technical document "Tr-87-171 Methodology for Software Reliability Prediction," which is one of the first documents to address prediction of software reliability before the software is coded, as opposed to estimating reliability while the software is being tested (which is how many of the reliability models are used). This document was prepared in a similar manner to the "DOD-STD 217F Reliability Prediction of Electronic Parts," which predicts hardware reliability for electronic components. Data were collected on a cross section of software programs and analyzed until some previously intangible software characteristic could be quantified. The software characteristics that were quantified in this document were:

1. Application type
2. Development environment
3. Requirements and design representation
4. Software implementation

The reliability prediction is equal to the product of these predictive metrics, which are composed of the following measures.

The application type is based on the end-user function to be performed by the software. Some examples of applications may be database management systems (DBMS), real-time operating system, diagnostic, development tools, batch, communications, satellite, strategic systems, tactical systems, and commercial avionics.

The development environment is considered to be either (1) organic mode, (2) semidetached mode, or (3) embedded mode. The organic mode is a small group of developers who are familiar with the end-user environment. The semidetached mode occurs when the development group has a wide variety of experience and familiarity with the required function of the software to be developed. The embedded mode occurs when the development group must develop a system that has tight cost and requirements constraints. The development environment metric is based on which of the three environments most accurately represents the development group at hand.

The requirement and design metrics consist of a subset of metrics. These are anomaly management, traceability, and quality review results. The product of these three submetrics equals the requirement and design metric.

The anomaly metric is the degree to which fault tolerance exists in the system. It is evaluated by using checklists.

The traceability metric is a measure of how well the software matches the requirements to which it was designed. This is determined by calculating the total number of requirements to the total number of traceable requirements.

The quality review results metric is determined by using a checklist. The total number of requirements met by the checklist identified in the system divided by the total number of requirements, minus the total number of discrepancy reports identified by the checklist, equals the quality review metric. These discrepancy reports are generated based on the use of a checklist during reviews that attempt to measure accuracy, completeness, consistency, and autonomy of the requirements defined.

The software implementation metric is the product of the language type metric, program size metric, modularity metric, extent of reuse metric, complexity metric, and standards review results metric.

The language type metric is equal to 1.4 for assembly and 1 for a higher-order language. For mixed languages it is equal to the percentage of each language multiplied by the respective metric value. This metric is intended to account for the assumption that assembly language is more dense.

The program size metric ranges from programs with less than 10,000 lines of code to programs with greater than 100,000 lines of code. In many software systems being developed today, there are many times over 100,000 lines of code being developed.

The modularity metric ranges from less than 200 lines of code per module to greater than 3000 lines of code per module. On many recent government contracts, it is required that there be less than an average of 200 lines of code per module.

The extent of reuse metric is determined by empirical data in a look-up table.

The complexity metric is determined by calculating the average complexity of each module of the software. (See Chapters 9 and 10 for more information on this.)

The standards review results metric is determined by dividing the number of modules in the software by the number of modules minus the number of modules with severe discrepancies. These discrepancies may be:

1. Not designed from top down.
2. Module is not independent.
3. Module processing is not independent.
4. Module is not documented well.
5. Module has more than one entrance or exit.
6. Module has minimum of global data.
7. There are no duplicate functions.

The RADC standard reviews results is extremely similar to the design structure metric discussed in both the IEEE and Software Quality Indicators documents.

The predictive metrics were developed based on empirical data collected by RADC. There are probably other metrics that may also be predictive but have not been researched or implemented by RADC as yet. Some of the metrics indicate that the data collected were most likely from older projects, which were smaller in size than those being developed today and in lower level languages. However, this document is a first stab at predicting the reliability of software before it is finished being developed. The hardware reliability prediction standard for electronic parts is continually updated as technology changes. A predictive metric guidelines such as this one would also have to be updated with technology to be usable.

One advantage to a prediction metric such as this one is that if all developers use it, the end result may not be as valuable as the relative results. The government (or any other customer) could use a predictive metric such as this for predicting reliability relative to other projects or contractors. The disadvantage to this predictive metric is that it is still not determined how accurate it is. See Chapter 8 for more information on using this model.

IBM has developed an approach to measuring the software process technology that is based on 15 attributes that are scored from 0 to 16. The sum of the score is then multiplied by 100/240 to normalize for an ideal score of 100. Their data have shown that as the software process technology metric increases, productivity and error rates are lowered. The 15 attributes are:

1. Inspections
2. Structured programming
3. Structured design language
4. Function model
5. State machine model
6. Network model
7. Structured specification language
8. Unit testing
9. Integration testing
10. Function testing
11. Systems testing
12. Performance and limit testing
13. User testing
14. Management technology education
15. Nonmanagement technology education

The Software Engineering Institute at the Carnegie Mellon University has developed a set of criteria for determining the level in which an organization has a software development process defined. According to the SEI criteria, a score of 1 indicates that there is no defined process at all for developing software. A level of 5 indicates that a process is defined in place and that the process is continually monitored and improved upon. At this writing, a score of 1 is not uncommon and a score of 2 is very common.

NASA Goddard Space Flight Center sponsored an organization in 1987 called the Software Engineering Laboratory, which is composed of NASA, the University of Maryland, and Computer Sciences Corporation. The objectives of SEL are to understand the software development process, identify methodologies and tools that measure the process, and apply successful development practices. Since 1978 the SEL has attempted to quantify characteristics of the software development process in order to improve the process. They have identified characteristics of the development process, applied methodologies and approaches to portions of the process that indicated a need for improvement, and assessed their methodologies and approaches by using various metrics.

The SEL at various times has identified a problem area with respect to cost, productivity, and reliability such as software rework or documentation, applied methodologies to improve the problem area, and then used metrics that were specific to the problem area to monitor the process. This cycle has been continued as new problem areas are defined.

The SEL has implemented various reliability models while attempting to measure progress. Some interesting findings by the SEL are that there seemed to be a relationship between reliability and technology. This was also found by IBM as discussed earlier. SEL also found that a relatively small amount of the development expense was attributed to coding, but a large amount was spent in rework and documentation. Methodologies were implemented to improve the cost due to rework, and documentation and metrics were used to measure the improvement.

4.2   ALLOCATIONS FOR SYSTEM AND SOFTWARE RELIABILITY

One reason for predicting and measuring the reliability of software is to determine the reliability of a system. Until recent years, the system reliability prediction and allocations for government software were based on the assumption that the reliability of software would be close to or equal to 1. It was realized years ago as software became a larger part of the system that this assumption was no longer acceptable. Methods for determining the reliability of software in the same units of measure as defined for hardware reliability were sought after. If software reliability could be calculated in terms of a failure rate, then the system failure rate could be determined essentially by adding the hardware and software failure rates.

In 1977 the government began requiring on some contracts that software reliability be addressed. Since then, how it is addressed has varied from contract to contract. In recent years it has been required that allocations for system reliability be determined and that software development procedures be implemented to ensure software reliability. The one variable that still exists today is how to measure the software reliability part of the system. Some of the more popular reliability models discussed in Chapter 8 have been used; unfortunately, most of them must be used as estimators, or as the software is being tested, as opposed to the requirements phase when the allocation is made. Historical data from previous generations of similar software has been used as a guideline for prediction. Lines-of-code estimates have also been used with some assumption of what the errors per line of code estimate will be. The RADC document discussed is one method for predicting reliability at this phase.

Unfortunately, adding the failure rates of software and hardware assumes that hardware and software failures are independent, and that there are no hardware failures due to software and vice versa. Some models have been investigated that do not attempt to separate the hardware and software failures. Instead, they attempt to measure the system reliability as a whole as opposed to the sum of the parts. George Stark of the Mitre Corporation developed a model used at NASA that uses a semi-Markov process to evaluate system reliability. The model assumes that the system is in one of six states: (1) good, (2) hardware degraded, (3) software degraded, (4) multiple degraded, (5) hardware critical, and (6) software critical. The inputs to the model are the number of transitions from one state to another and the time spent in each state. Stark defines the paths that are possible from state to state, and the probabilities for each possible transition are computed and solved for in the transition matrix. The reliability is computed as the probability of transitioning from a good state. The availability is then computed as the probability of either a hardware or software critical state.

The author has found that one of the most effective means of determining a system allocation for software prior to development or during developing is to accumulate the number of software and hardware trouble reports and any downtime associated with them. When developing new software, historical data on this metric can be used until real data are available.

There are various software reliability demonstration tests discussed in Chapter 5 that may be used to verify that a software reliability allocation has been met. One of these may also be used to verify that a system reliability allocation has been met.

SUMMARY

Some of the methods for measuring and improving software reliability that have been addressed by either government or industry are:

1. *Design structure metrics:* measurement of the design approach, complexity, and independence of the software design.
2. *Design completeness metrics:* measurement of the ability of the software to perform intended requirements and functions completely.
3. *Process metrics:* measurement of the management, cost-effectiveness, and design tradeoffs of software.
4. *Product metrics:* measurement of the characteristics of the software that are specific to the product developed. Design completeness and structure metrics are a subset of product metrics.
5. *Reliability modeling and prediction:* reliability prediction methods based on empirical data have been developed by the government to be used very early in the life cycle. The accuracy of the predictions are being researched. Many software reliability models that are used in later phases of development have been used with varying results.

Some of the approaches toward measuring system reliability have been to measure the failure rates of hardware and software and sum them, or to measure the system reliability as a whole as opposed to a sum of the parts. System allocations have been performed in the past with the assumption that software reliability was equal to 1. Now system allocations are including software as a reliability component.

REFERENCES

Air Force Systems Command. *Software Quality Insight,* AFSCP 800-14, January 1987.

Dependability Evaluation of Integrated Hardware/Software Systems. IEEE Transactions on Reliability, New York, October 1987.

Grady, R., and Caswell, D. *Software Metrics: Establishing a Company Wide Program.* Hewlett-Packard Company, Prentice-Hall, Englewood Cliffs, NJ, 1987.

IEEE Guide for the Use of IEEE Standard Dictionary of Measures to Produce Reliable Software, IEEE Standard 982.2. IEEE Publications, New York, 1988.

IEEE Standard Dictionary of Measures to Produce Reliable Software, IEEE Standard 982.1. IEEE Publications, New York, 1988.

Proceedings of the Eleventh Annual Software Engineering Workshop, SEL-86-006, Greenbelt, MD, December 1986.

RADC-TR-87-171 Methodology For Software Prediction. Air Force Systems Command, Griffiss Air Force Base, New York, 1987.

---------------- CHAPTER 5 ----------------

Factors that Affect
Software Reliability

There are many development factors that determine how reliable the software will be. These factors for the most part are difficult to quantify in tangible terms. However, some attempts by Rome Air Development Center (RADC) and the Air Force Systems Command (AFSC) have been made to do so (see Chapters 4 and 8). Thomas McCabe of McCabe and Associates has also attempted to quantify the effect of some of these design factors. The presence and degree to which these factors exist in a given development project have a relationship with the software reliability. Chapter 5 addresses the factors, their relationship with reliability, and, if applicable, how these factors may be measured or implemented.

5.1 METHODOLOGIES AND TOOLS

Some of the methodologies and tools that may affect software reliability follow.

5.1.1 Structured Design, Code, Test, and Maintenance

Structured design is characterized by a design that is defined before code is developed. Structured design usually has a minimum of global variables (shared data) and usually utilizes local data passed within parameter statements. Structured design is usually modular in that a given module will perform exactly one function completely. If that module requires a change, then it should have a minimal impact on the rest of the software.

Structured code is code that adheres to the same characteristics just listed. Structured testing is an approach to testing the software as efficiently as possible. The design and code should already be structured to some extent to perform structured testing. The structured testing approach maximizes test coverage while minimizing the number of test cases; see chapter 10 for more information. Structured maintenance is an approach toward maintaining software so as not to introduce new errors due to a maintenance action and to verify that the maintenance action is successfully eliminating the error or errors. It depends heavily on the software being well documented and structured.

5.1.2 Pseudocode and Flow Diagrams

Pseudocode is used for detailed design. It resembles code and English, hence its name pseudocode (false code). A form of pseudocode is product descriptive language (PDL). The PDL may be formatted or even compiled as a detailed level design tool. Pseudocode may have a direct impact on the reliability of the code because it is the design for which the code is developed. An absence of PDL or pseudocode probably represents the absence of a structured design. Flowcharts are a tool for top-level design and are the basis for the detailed design. Flowcharts are a necessary input for many structured design, code, test, and maintenance analyses.

5.1.3 Tools for Designing, Coding, Testing, Maintaining, and Tracing Code to Requirements

These tools may or may not be automated. Pseudocode and flowcharts are design tools. The PDL or pseudocode is also a coding tool, especially if it is a formattable automated tool. Testing tools may include tools to indicate the structural test paths, functional test paths, and algorithm test paths (see Chapter 10 for more on these types of tests), as well as tools for automatically executing the test cases. Maintenance tools may be tools that allow for a correction to the software with a minimal risk of adversely affecting code that already functions correctly. Tools for tracing code to requirements would ensure that every requirement is addressed, that every requirement is addressed correctly, and that no requirement is addressed more than once.

5.1.4 Progress and Status Reporting and Error Tracking

Progress and status reporting may be automated. It is necessary to track process data, product data, and error data on a regular and up-to-date basis. Status reporting allows for decision making based on the results indicated by these three sources of data. Progress and status reporting must be present to some degree in order to effectively implement any of the models discussed in Chapter 8.

5.1.5 Design and Code Walkthroughs

The presence of effective design and code walkthroughs is directly related to the reliability of software. For walkthroughs to be effective there should generally be three to five people present, including software development and quality assurance. An agenda must be determined prior to the walkthrough, and there must be a reasonable time limit as well as action items taken. Each participant should review the code or design prior to the walkthrough. Things to avoid during a walkthrough are an unorganized agenda, too many or too few participants, and an unclear criteria for the objective of the walkthrough.

5.1.6 Formal Reviews

Formal reviews are a necessary part of the software design process and are intended to minimize ambiguities in requirements and potential design and coding errors.

5.2 LEARNING FACTOR

The experience and training of the development team may have an impact on software reliability. One interesting point to note is that structured design techniques that have a very direct relationship to maintainability and reliability have not be used extensively until the past decade. For this reason, it may not be safe to assume that more experience is better. The degree to which each of the personnel interact with each other as a development team will probably have a more direct impact than the overall experience level of the team.

5.3   ORGANIZATION

The type of organization that is developing the software may have a direct effect on the software reliability. An organization that has internal objectives and requirements for reliability may make it policy to design for software that not only meets the customer's contractual requirements (if there are any) but may exceed those requirements in order to remain competitive or even to remain in business.

According to a survey conducted by Donald Reifer Consultants and the American Society for Quality Control, only 7% of 98 companies surveyed were implementing or had implemented software reliability models. (These companies were for the most part from the aerospace industry.) The low percentage could be due to the facts that there is not one accepted method of modeling software reliability, the methods that do exist are relatively new and not completely validated, and software engineering itself is a relatively new field. In any case, for any organization to know how to produce reliability software, it must first know how reliable its current software is and how effective its current practices are.

The industry may dictate the acceptable levels of reliability in software and also the methods for predicting and estimating software reliability. Government contractors in general are finding themselves with requirements for improving, estimating, predicting, and allocating software reliability. This includes the defense, energy, transportation, and space industries. Other industries such as the medical and financial software industries are being guided by other external factors such as the possibility or probability of a lawsuit.

5.4   DOCUMENTATION

There are two types of software documentation. The first type is the documentation actually contained in the software code itself. The second type is the documentation external to the software, which indicates how the software will be developed and also aids in maintaining the software.

The documentation that should be contained in the software code itself consists of the following:

1. The name of module and the location of the module within the hierarchy tree.
2. The function of the module. Ideally one only complete function should performed by each module. This should be described.
3. The configuration history. The dates the module was created, the detailed design was complete, the detailed design reviewed, the code completed, the code reviewed, the unit testing completed, the unit test plans and procedures reviewed, the integration testing completed, and any maintenance action after integration testing should be documented in order to aid in source control and also to aid the developer or maintainer in making changes to the design or code.
4. A detailed design consisting of PDL or pseudocode. This should be present so that during the coding, testing, and maintaining phases, the software development person may immediately refer to the detailed design. This design would also be changed if necessary when conditions require it.
5. One piece of information that could also exist in the code itself is the structural complexity of the design.
6. The author has found that including the actual requirements of the module in the code itself allows for immediate traceability to the requirements. It also aids the maintainer (or maintainers) later when correcting the code. The author includes the requirements for the module in the code itself and numbers them. Then the numbers are associated with the segments of code to assure that all requirements are coded and that none are coded more than once. When the requirements are changed, this documentation changes with it. The same action is then taken at levels higher than the module to ensure that each module addresses all requirements at a higher level and that each requirement is addressed only once.

Some of the external documentation developed is as follows:

1. *A configuration management (CM) plan:* This plan indicates how the source configuration will be maintained. It is necessary in order to

have traceability for maintenance changes and also to keep source versions under control.

2. *Quality assurance (QA) plan:* This plan indicates how the quality assurance function, which is usually independent of development, will assure that the final software quality is acceptable.
3. *Software development plan:* This plan indicates how the development organization will go about developing software. It contains information about the facilities, the organization, the methodologies and tools used, and any other information specific to how the software will be developed.
4. *Software requirements specification:* This documentation contains the specifications for how each of the requirements will be implemented.
5. *Software design specification:* This documentation contains the top-level design specifications for the software.
6. *Software test plans and procedures:* These documents contain information on how each module will be tested and the procedures (inputs) used for testing them. It also includes how the system as a whole will be tested and the procedures (inputs) for testing the system.

There is clearly quite a bit of documentation that needs to be kept for software development. One of the experiences of software development people, particularly government contractors, is that more time may be spent developing the documentation than in developing the software. The existence alone of this documentation will not assure that software is developed correctly: only effective documentation will accomplish this.

5.5   COMPLEXITY

Structural complexity is based on the logic paths of each of the modules. A branch in logic in software is represented by if–then–else, while, do, for, loop, case, repeat, if–then, and any other statement that causes the logic of the software to have more than one possible path. The structural complexity is essentially the number of these branches plus one. This is a simplification of structural complexity; it is further discussed in Chapter 10. According to Thomas McCabe, the complexity is related to the testability of the code, which is related to the quality. This means that the higher the complexity, the harder it is to test and therefore the greater the chance of sufficient testing not being performed. McCabe suggests that the structural complexity for each unit or module should not exceed 11 except when there is a case statement or when there are exception handlers for checking the status of I/O or other operations. What happens when the complexity exceeds 11? The author has not experienced any particular event when the complexity exceeds 11. The author, as well as other authors, has found a relationship between complexity and reliability; however, structural complexity is a better indicator when used in conjunction with functional complexity.

Functional complexity is based on the required functions that a segment of code must perform. Ideally, one module should perform one and only one function completely. There should be one set of cohesive inputs and one set of cohesive outputs, which are all related to each other and the function to be performed. The author has found that the need to develop modules that perform exactly one function (not less than one function either) outweighs the necessity to develop a module strictly on the basis of structural complexity. Many times, however, modules that are high in functional complexity are also high in structural complexity. Software modules low in functional complexity may still be high in structural complexity.

5.6 ENVIRONMENT

The end-user environment has a direct impact on how reliable the software will be. Some aspects of the end-user environment that must be addressed when designing the software are:

5.6.1 Interfaces with Software, Hardware, and Humans

The degree to which the software interfaces with other software, with various hardware, and with humans will have an impact on software reliability. Software with extensive interface with other software will require verification of those interfaces over and above verification of the software function itself. Software with extensive and various hardware interfaces may be prone to changing requirements due to changing hardware. Software with extensive user interface will require a user-friendly design that is tolerant to user error and is also designed for the end user's capabilities.

5.6.2   Training of End Users

Software that has a human interface will require some training of the end user. The more user-friendly the software is, the more likely the user will not make user errors and will not require as much training or as extensive a user manual. In any case, the educational abilities of the end user should be reflected in the design of the software to avoid user errors. There is a fine line between what is a software error and what is a user error. A good rule of thumb is to consider the profile of the average user, the type of error that was made (i.e., did it cause loss of data or whatever), whether or not the user specifically misused the software or intentionally performed functions incorrectly, and whether or not the error was avoidable by the user. On some safety-critical systems, the software may have to be designed to avoid 100% of the user errors that would be made by the small percentile of users who are very inexperienced or the small percentile of users who are extremely experienced and able to misuse the software.

5.6.3   Variability of Input Data

There are some test cases that may not be easily testable in a laboratory environment. There are some ranges of input data that may only be simulated and therefore will never be completely tested until the system is developed and in use.

5.7   PRESENCE OF PROTOTYPING

Software prototyping in technical terms is the building of a shell, partial system, or modification of an existing system in order to provide a physical model for which to develop requirements and design. A prototype may have no real functioning capability.

Software prototyping may be done in a different language, such as LISP, or a language that compiles quickly so that changes and updates to the prototype may be made on the fly. Prototypes may also be an older existing software program that is modified to display enhancements. Prototypes may also be developed in the same language as the software that is to be developed. They may be partial functions of the system.

Prototyping occurs between the concept phase and the detailed design phase. It is an iterative process and should generally be completed before the detailed design begins for the software program in which it is prototyping. In some organizations the marketing or field personnel may develop the prototype, as opposed to the software engineers. Prototyping is often an excellent tool for refining requirements, and minimizing ambiguous and incomplete requirements. This is an effort to reduce the number of errors that will eventually be detected and attributed to unclear, incomplete, and even incorrect requirements. It may also be successful in exposing implicit requirements, which are those requirements that are assumed to be understood by the development team but are not.

Normally, prototyping is performed when there is an extensive user interface and the requirements of the user may not be clearly defined on paper. Prototyping is also performed when performance is a critical issue. A prototype may allow the development team to determine whether a particular design will meet a given set of performance criteria. Prototyping is also useful when a brand new concept or idea is being developed and it is not entirely clear if the concept is even feasible.

The prototype may be reviewed by the internal development team, by the customer, or by some group of users that represent the average end user of the software. It is essential that someone representing the typical end user review the prototype.

The prototype may be throw-away (if it is developed in a different language then it will have to be), or it may be built upon.

The advantages of prototyping with respect to reliability are that the prototype may minimize software errors that are due to unclear, incomplete, or changing requirements. If prototyping is performed early in the development process and is an iterative process where the customer or a representative of the typical end user reviews the prototype and develops requirements from it, then it may have a substantial impact on reliability.

One disadvantage of prototyping is that a prototype may so closely resemble functioning software that a customer (or management) may be misled into believing the software is already in the coding phase, as opposed to the requirements phase. The customer as well as management may expect a faster turnaround time because of it. It is suggested that an internal marketing team or internal line of business personnel review the prototype to avoid this problem. For example, if the software is for the financial industry, a team of typical end users such as tellers may be utilized to review the prototype and provide recommendations.

Another disadvantage of prototyping with a very direct impact on software reliability is that if a prototype is developed to be throw-away, it *must* be thrown away. This means that the prototype should not be developed upon. The reason for this is that a prototype is developed quickly, many times with no development guidelines. If the prototype becomes a real product, it may be based on a poor basic design. This will negatively affect the reliability of the software.

5.8   REQUIREMENTS TRANSLATION AND TRACEABILITY

There exist two areas where potential software errors may be introduced to the software. The first area is in defining the requirements to a level that is detailed enough, complete enough, clear enough, and explicit enough for the developer to translate, and the second area of error is in actually translating those requirements.

Errors commonly made in developing the requirements are:

1. Failure to make the requirements detailed enough. When requirements do not contain sufficient detail, the software engineer will most likely develop the code based on his or her assumption of what the top-level requirements specify. Many times the customer assumes that the developer understands the next level of detail when in fact he or she may not know precisely what is not explicitly stated.
2. Failure to include all of the required features. The reason for this is that the customer may again assume that the developer knows what is explicitly not stated.
3. Failure to make requirements clear and understood by the average software engineer or programmer, who may or may not have complete understanding of the end user environment. This problem is usually due again to assumptions about what is explicit and what is implicitly understood about the software to be developed.

Errors made commonly when translating the requirements are:

1. Failure to address all of the requirements. The requirements do not necessarily have a one-to-one relationship with the hierarchy or structure tree for the software. A given set of requirements may require *x* number of modules to implement. It must be verified that all of the requirements are addressed by the modules as a whole.
2. Addressing a given requirement more than once. Fortunately, this

generally occurs less often than missing a requirement. This requirements error may be due to more than one person designing to the same requirements or to ineffective breakdown of the requirements among the hierarchy structure.

3. Failure to translate the requirement correctly. It is not uncommon for requirements that are clear and complete to be translated incorrectly anyway. This could be due to a lack of developer capability.

5.9 TEST METHODOLOGY

There are at least four ways in which software testing is performed. Each of these has a different impact on reliability and cost.

5.9.1 Independent Validation and Verification

Independent validation and verification (IV&V) means that the testing group is completely independent functionally of the development organization. They may not even be employed by the same company. The IV&V testing is performed from the black box point of view. The testers are testing from the end user's functional point of view, as opposed to the developer's point of view. The advantage to IV&V with respect to reliability is that the testers are likely to find errors that the development team may have missed due to lack of line of business experience or due to blindness from familiarity. The disadvantage of this type of testing may be in familiarizing the independent testers with the software and the turnaround time involved if the testers are not a part of the same company as the development organization.

5.9.2 Distribution of Responsibilities

Design, code, and test are distributed to each member of the development organization so that person A may design module A, code module B, and test module C. Person B may design module B, code module C, and test module A. Person C may design module C, code module A, and test module B. This type of testing can be used in conjunction with IV&V. The advantage to this type of testing with respect to reliability is that all members of the development team are exposed to various portions of the entire software system. Turnover in manpower may be more comfortably accommodated by this kind of testing environment. Also, there may be less bias in testing and errors due to blindness from familiarity. If this author had to pick a testing scenario suitable for total quality management, this would be it.

One disadvantage of this type of testing is the time required for hand-off between each of the phases on each module. Each person needs time to become familiar with the requirements of the new module in addition to the design and code of that module. If the development team is composed of temporary help or short-term contracting software engineers or programmers, this may not be the most efficient use of their time.

5.9.3   Independent Developers, Testers, and Coders

This type of testing approach assumes that one group of personnel will always design, another group will always code, another group will always test, and another will always maintain.

The advantage of this type of testing, with respect to reliability, is that fewer personnel need to become familiar with the requirements of the software, and probably fewer who will need to interface with the customer to translate requirements. Each of the groups of personnel will be specialized in the fields of design, code, test, and maintenance, and this may reduce bias as well as blindness due to familiarity. The major advantage of this approach is that it can be the fastest.

The disadvantage of this testing approach is that if the designers do not interpret the requirements correctly, it will probably be reflected throughout the entire system instead of contained in part of it. Also, this approach does not necessarily allow for growth as a software engineer, and if the developers have no choice as to which function (design, code, or test) they must perform, they may become bored.

5.9.4   No Independent Testing

This testing approach assumes that person A will design, code, test, and possibly maintain the same portion of code from beginning to end.

The advantage of this testing approach is that the developer may feel a sense of ownership. There is also no turnaround time between design, code, and test.

The disadvantage of this approach is that there may not be an independent review of the design and code. Any problems that do exist may take a while to surface and may therefore be more costly to fix. An obvious disadvantage also occurs if the person leaves the company or even moves on to a different position. Some people may also become bored with the product they have developed and so may be less likely to find errors in it.

5.10   MAINTENANCE

The existence of documentation, standards, and methodologies for software maintenance will have a very direct impact on the software reliability. Software that is difficult to maintain is prone to errors generated during maintenance that were not inherently contained in the software.

Documentation contained in the source code itself is the best sort of prevention of maintenance errors and also the best way to expedite software maintenance. The PDL contained in the code as well as the configuration history and the description of functional requirements is critical in aiding the software maintainer; so are useful and precise comment statements.

Another piece of documentation that is useful for testing the change made during the maintenance phase is the flow diagram. Let us assume that a maintainer has made a modification to a module in an attempt to fix a reported fault. Once the correction is made, the maintainer will need to verify that the change has fixed the problem that was discovered. The testing does not end here, however. The maintainer must also assure that no new errors were introduced due to this change and that previously correct code is still correct. The best ways to find the test paths that are affected by the change are with a flow diagram of the logic of the module as well as a higher level hierarchy or structure chart of the flow of control to that module.

Standards that may exist for maintenance may include the types of documentation just described as well as procedures for reviewing maintenance actions and the methodologies for testing the maintenance action. See Chapter 10 for more information on these procedures.

5.11   SCHEDULE

The schedule obviously is a parameter that has a direct effect on the reliability of the software. Unfortunately, many of the models available for predicting software reliability cannot account for the effect of the schedule and changes in schedule on software reliability. There is a natural inclination for management to fix reliability by adding more people—unfortunately, after the damage may have already been done with respect to reliability. John Musa indicates that there is some initial benefit in doing this; however, after some breakpoint the reliability return diminishes with increased manpower.

Schedule has an intangible impact on reliability in other ways. Structured design, code, test, and maintenance require that more effort be exerted in the initial requirements and design phases than in the later phases. Schedules, however, are often developed to allow for the most time to be spent on coding or testing. This may cause the design effort to be short-changed, resulting in more requirements and design errors discovered later on in the development process. It seems to be natural for development personnel as well as management to feel that the major milestone is having the code exist, even if that code may not meet requirements and may be designed poorly.

5.12   LANGUAGE

Higher-order languages such as Ada, C, and PASCAL are commonly known to be more suitable for structured development than the lower-order languages such as assembly language. Structured development can very well be accomplished using a language such as assembly language; however, when using a higher-order language it is much more difficult *not* to use a structured approach.

5.13   EXISTENCE OF SIMILAR SOFTWARE

When it is applicable, the existence of similar software may have an impact on the reliability of the software. This applies for the most part to off-the-shelf software when there exists software similar in nature that may become a physical model to develop from. If the company's goal is to produce a software package that is better than some other product, the existence of that product within the development environment will probably have an effect on the reliability of the software to be developed.

5.14   QUALITATIVE CHARACTERISTICS OF SOFTWARE

There are various software development characteristics that may influence software reliability. These design parameters vary in the degree to which they are related to software reliability. Figure 5.1 illustrates each of the design parameters. Those parameters that have a tendency to op-

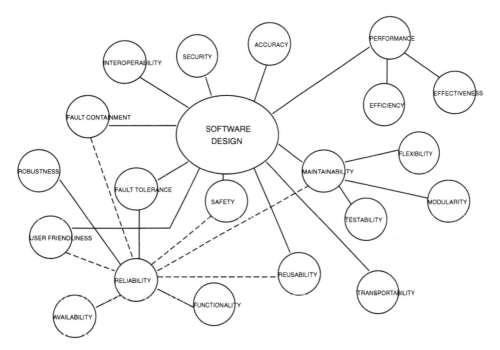

Figure 5.1 Software design parameters.

pose the objectives for reliable software, such as performance, are located the farthest from reliability. Those design parameters that are closely associated with software reliability, such as user friendliness, are located close to reliability. The diagram also shows the relationship of each design parameter with each other.

Any of these parameters may or may not exist on any particular development project. For example, security, interoperability, transportability, safety, or user friendliness may not be pertinent to programs that do not require security mechanisms, do not have an extensive software interface, will never be used on another platform, will never be safety critical, and have a negligible user interface. The design parameters are discussed as follows.

Fault containment is the ability of the software to keep the effects of a software error contained to a minimal portion of the code. Fault containment is best visualized with database design. If we were developing a program that stored and manipulated large amounts of data, our objective would be to assure that if an error is made writing to that database, the error is contained so that the entire database is not affected.

This containment would be accomplished by requiring I/O status checks on every statement that writes to the database and error messages indicating when a write error has occurred.

Interoperability is the ability for the software to function with other software.

Security is the ability for the software to protect itself from misuse. Protecting against misuse may include anything from password protection to prevention of viruses, to even more drastic measures of protection that cause a breakdown of the violator's user information if an illegal attempt is made on the system by that user.

Accuracy is the ability for the software to produce results that are within the tolerance expected. Accuracy is a big issue with financial and medical software. An algorithm used for computing the interest on an account must be as accurate for $1 as it is for $1 million.

Performance is a function of efficiency and effectiveness.

Efficiency is the ability of the software to perform its intended function with the minimum amount of resources necessary. The author previously described performance as tending to be an opposing force for development of reliable software. This is not always true, of course, but when it is the case it is probably due to maintenance. Many times the fastest, most efficient algorithm may not be easily maintainable by the average software engineer or programmer. Maintenance attempts may introduce new errors that adversely affect software reliability.

Effectiveness is the degree to which the software performs its required function and how valid the results are.

Maintainability is a function of flexibility, modularity, and documentation.

Flexibility is the ability of the software to be updated with relative ease to changes in technology and requirements. One example the author always gives her students of structured design is this: You are required to develop code that will find the largest value of from 1 to 1000 integers. You could write your code so that it works for exactly 1 to 1000 integers, or you could write your code so that it will find the largest value from any number of integers (including no integers). Each approach would provide the same end result, which is the largest integer. However, if the requirements were to be adjusted, then the second approach would need no modifications.

Modularity is the degree to which each unit of the software is independent of the other units, as well as the degree of cohesiveness of the module. A module is cohesive if it performs exactly one function completely. For example, if a module converted degrees Fahrenheit to degrees Celsius and also converted miles to kilometers it would not be cohesive. The input for the temperature conversion is in degrees Fahrenheit. The input for the distance conversion is in miles. The output of the temperature conversion is in degrees Celsius. The output of the distance conversion is in kilometers. The inputs are not related to each other or bound together and neither are the outputs.

If the design were modular, there would be one module for the temperature conversion and one module for distance conversion.

A design is also modular if the extent and amount of global variables are minimized. If a module utilized global data that are shared by many other modules, then it could be difficult to make modifications to this module for fear of having a global effect on the data. Local variables allow for easier fault isolation and also allow for increased fault containment.

Transportability is the ability for the software to be usable on other platforms.

Reusability is the ability to use portions of the code again for other software systems. Reusability may have either a positive or negative effect on software reliability, depending on whether the reusable software is really reusable. If code is to be reused and requires extensive modifications or does not perform the intended function precisely, there could be a negative impact. Obviously, code that is reused that does perform the intended function precisely will affect the reliability of the new software, depending on how reliable the reused software is.

Availability is the percentage of time that the software is functioning. Availability is a function of fault tolerance, reliability, and maintainability.

Safety is the ability for the software to perform safety-critical or mission-critical functions. Safety may not necessarily be directly related to reliability. A function could be performed that does not cause a safety hazard but does not perform according to the requirements.

Robustness is the ability of the software to function under hostile conditions, or under a wide variety of inputs, or under the maximum or minimum range of inputs.

User friendliness is the ability of the software to conform to supporting documentation, to prevent the user from making errors that will cause a fault or failure, and to be easily teachable to users.

Fault tolerance is the ability of the software to recover from its own fault or failure and continue functioning.

Table 5.1 Factors That Affect Software Reliability

Factor	Effect
Methodologies and tools	Structured approaches to design, code, test, and maintenance may improve it.
Learning factor	Total experience as well as experience with structured methodologies may improve it.
Organization	The organization's philosophy, guidelines and standards may affect it.
Documentation	The source code, technical references, and development plans may affect it.
Environment	The end-user environment and the ease of modeling that environment may affect it.
Complexity	The structural and functional complexity may affect it.
Prototyping	The existence of effective prototyping during the concept, requirements, and design phase may improve it.
Requirements traceability	The effectiveness with which requirements are translated and traced during development may affect it.
Test methodology	The methodology used to test and verify the software system as a whole may affect it.
Maintenance	The manner in which maintenance actions are implemented may affect it.
Schedule	The schedule and resource constraints will affect it.
Language	The use of a higher-order language may affect it.
Similar software	The existence of software that is similar and can be used for modeling purposes may affect it.
Qualitative	These characteristics include maintainability, reusability, safety, fault tolerance, fault containment, secu-

Table 5.1   (Continued)

Factor	Effect
	rity, accuracy, portability, flexibility, performance, and user friendliness.

5.15   TRADEOFFS OF DESIGN PARAMETERS

The development parameters described in this chapter will require a tradeoff with respect to each other and reliability. For example, an airline reservation system demands security to prevent the airline from going out of business, it requires availability to keep customers content, and it also requires some degree of accuracy so that correct reservations and prices are produced. In this case, the need for security, availability, and accuracy must be determined and tradeoffs performed so that each of the objectives is accomplished within schedule and cost.

SUMMARY

There are many factors involved in designing software. Many of these factors have a very direct impact on software reliability. The factors that are known to have the strongest relationship with reliable software are summarized in Table 5.1.

REFERENCES

American Society for Quality Control, *Software Quality Survey,* Software Quality Technical Committee. Milwaukee, WI, 1987.

DeMarco, Tom. *Concise Notes on Software Engineering,* Yourdon Press, New York, 1979.

McCabe, Thomas. *Structural Testing,* McCabe & Associates, Columbia, MD, 1985.

Musa, J., Iannino, A., and Okumoto, K. *Software Reliability Measurement, Prediction, Application,* McGraw-Hill, New York, 1987.

RADC-TR-87-171 Methodology for Software Prediction, Air Force Systems Command, Griffiss Air Force Base, New York, 1987.

CHAPTER 6

Software Reliability
Terms and Definitions

This chapter defines some of the terms that are used specifically in Chapters 7 and 8. Various types of software errors, software tests, and assumptions about the distribution of errors over time are discussed.

6.1 TYPES OF SOFTWARE ERRORS

There are three general types of software errors: (1) coding and logic errors, (2) requirements errors, and (3) errors due to some other external interface or influence. The requirements errors are described in detail in Chapter 7. The various types of coding errors are described as follows.

Recurring Error

This is an error that actually is repeated in more than one place in the software code. For example, if an error was detected and corrected, but that same error was made elsewhere and not corrected, then it will eventually recur. Would you consider this recurring error to be one error or more than one? The best answer to that question is to consider how many repairs were needed to eliminate all occurrences of the error. If they were all corrected the first time the error was detected, then you may count this as one error; otherwise, count how many repairs were needed to eliminate the error and that may be the total number of errors. You will notice that this is essentially the same as counting the number of faults.

Note that the cause of recurring errors is generally a design that is not modular, hence the same code may be repeated throughout several modules, instead of being contained in one module. It may be a good idea to modularize the code that contained the recurring error.

Regenerated Error

This is an error that was not inherently contained in the software; instead, it was introduced into the software when a correction was made to fix another error. Regenerated errors should be counted as distinct errors, as they did not exist in the software until some maintenance action was initiated. These errors are due to incomplete verification of a maintenance action or a design that is not modular or structured and therefore lends itself to errors during the maintenance process.

Undetected Error

This is an error that is yet to be discovered or manifested as a fault. Keep in mind that you will never know with complete certainty how many of these actually exist. You may only approximate this.

Performance Error

This is an error that causes the software to not perform with its given resources as required. This performance may be stated in terms of response time, memory usage, CPU usages, and so on.

Data Error

This is an error caused by some piece of data not containing the correct value. This is a type of initialization error.

Initialization Error

This is an error due to either incorrect initialization of variables or a complete lack of initialization of variables. This author has experienced this type of error to be one of the most common coding errors. Unfortunately, it is also an error that many times is difficult to isolate.

6.2 CRITICALITY OF SOFTWARE ERRORS

The following is a classification of the criticality of errors, not unique to software.

1. *Catastrophic:* This type of error may cause an unsurpassable mission failure, a safety hazard, an injury, or loss of life. This type of error could be a failure that may have irreversible and catastrophic effects.
2. *Critical:* This type of error may cause a mission failure, unacceptable downtime, or loss of data. A critical error may also be an error that could potentially cause a lawsuit or a major loss of business.
3. *Moderate:* This type of error may cause undesirable downtime or partial loss of function, but it may be temporarily circumvented.
4. *Negligible:* This type of error has little effect on the functionality of the system except that it may be a nuisance to the user. It may never be fixed and still have a negligible effect on the overall system.
5. *All others:* Any type of error that cannot be categorized as described above. Those errors may be errors that are not due to the code itself.

If your intention is to measure or model software you will need to categorize each of the faults detected based on the preceding criteria. This is necessary so that an accurate picture may be drawn of the manpower required to fix the most critical errors first, the extent of damage that each of the errors may potentially have on the system, and the probability that a critical or catastrophic fault will be detected as opposed to any type of fault.

6.3 TYPES OF SOFTWARE TESTING

There are various types of testing that are performed on software at various points in the development phase. They are discussed next.

6.3.1   Testing Performed During the Life Cycle

1. *Unit testing*: Testing one compilable unit usually before that unit is integrated into the system. Sometimes it is not feasible or cost-effective to test a module before integrating it with a few more modules. This may happen if the range of inputs required for testing is so extensive that it may not be practically performed until the unit is integrated to some extent with some other part of the system.
2. *Integration testing*: Testing to verify the software as a whole. Ideally, if unit testing is thorough, this type of testing should find mostly interface errors and errors that would not have been easily found during unit testing.
3. *Acceptance testing*: Testing the software with the objective of verifying that the customers requirements are met. The customer may sometimes perform this test. Ideally, this test should be a final checkout and should uncover few errors.
4. *Regression testing*: Testing software that has been previously tested in an effort to uncover any errors that may have been due to maintenance actions, new code being developed, or improper configuration management or source control.

6.3.2   Software Tests with Specific Objectives

1. *Black box testing:* The easiest way to understand black box testing is to visualize a black box with a set of inputs coming into it and a set of outputs coming out of it. The black box test is performed without any knowledge of the code itself. Therefore, the tester is veiled from any bias that could result from having developed the code. The black box test verifies that the end-user requirements are met from the end user's point of view.
2. *White box testing:* This type of testing is, surprisingly enough, the opposite of black box testing. It is performed by personnel who have familiarity with the code and design and are testing from the developer's point of view. Both the white box and black box testing approaches must be implemented at some phase of the life cycle because there are some errors may only be found by a person who is close to the development of the design and code, and there are other errors that only a typical end user might uncover.

3. *Stress testing:* Attempts to break the system by stressing its available resources.

4. *Configuration testing:* Assures that the software functions under various device configurations.

5. *Load and performance testing:* Confirms that performance objectives are met. The performance of some response or some activity is measured and compared against what is required or can be tolerated by the user.

6. *Security testing:* Confirms that the system is not likely to be illegally accessed (at least not with known methods of illegal access!)

7. *Recovery testing:* Assures that the system can recover from some hardware or software malfunction without loss of data or function.

8. *Algorithm testing:* Verifies that an algorithm will not cause an error due to:

   (a) A maximum value being exceeded. This will happen if there is a divide-by-zero attempt, an exponent becomes too large, or the result of an algorithm is itself larger than the capacity of the system.

   (b) A minimum value being exceeded. This will happen if there is a square root attempt on a negative number, an exponent becomes too small, or the result of an algorithm is itself smaller than the smallest value of the system's capacity.

   (c) Logical conditions. If there are two conditions that are either AND-ed or OR-ed together, than there will be four distinct test cases for testing every possible combinations of conditions. See Chapter 10 for examples of logical testing.

   (d) Arithmetic operators. This testing assures that multiplication, division, addition, subtraction, and exponents are performed in the correct order.

6.4 SOFTWARE RELIABILITY TESTING

Now that we have seen the many types of software testing that may be performed on software, let us examine what types of testing could be used to validate the reliability of the software? There are at least five methods by which the reliability of the software may be validated. Three of these methods are deterministic, the result being either a pass or a fail. Five methods for verifying the reliability of the software are as follows:

Test 1: Data Collection and Verification During the Other Tests

The last but certainly not least method of testing the reliability of the software is to collect data during the other tests discussed during the life cycle and make measurements based on those data. Most of the models described in Chapter 8 may be used for this purpose.

The steps in the this type of reliability test, data collection, and verification testing are as follows:

1. Develop or enhance a software problem report that is practical and contains the basic inputs needed for the model or models to be used. See Chapters 7 and 8 for more information on the problem reporting.
2. Determine which model or models will be used to measure the software reliability. Guidelines for choosing these models are given in Chapter 8.
3. Implement an efficient and effective method for collecting the problem report data as well as process and product data (see Chapter 7).
4. Collect data during and after integration testing.
5. Input data on a regular basis into the model or models chosen.
6. Make estimates on a regular basis, such as the number of errors detected or corrected by some point in time, the rate of errors detected or corrected at some point in time, the testing time required to meet some reliability objective, the estimated number of residual errors, and other estimates.
7. Based on the results, make decisions as to the readiness of the software for release with respect to reliability. Determine whether additional test time will aid in meeting the objective.

Test 2: Beta

This type of testing is actually performed by a real end user. The end user may have received a special price for validating the software while concurrently using it for his or her own purposes. This is commonly done when brand new, off-the-shelf software is developed or when software is developed for a new application or end user. The objective is to have the end user test the software until it is ready for production or mass delivery.

Test 3: System Reliability Demonstration Test

This type of test would be on the system as a whole, including the hardware. There would be a required time for which the system would have to function (as it would in a real environment) without any repairs being made to the system. The number of faults found in a period of time would determine whether the system as a whole has passed or failed the reliability test. The criteria for pass and fail are discussed further after discussion of the next two types of tests.

Test 4: Software Demonstration Test Based on Testing Time

This reliability demonstration test is on software only and is performed over time. This type of test is applicable if the software is the major portion of the system being developed.

Test 5: Software Demonstration Test Based on Test Inputs

This type of reliability demonstration testing is also performed only on software; however, the test is not based on the passage of time. The test is based on sets of test inputs or test cases which are randomly selected and input.

In order to perform tests 3, 4, and 5, there must be three parameters that are determined prior to the test (probably by the customer). These parameters are:

1. The consumer risk α, which is the risk that software that is unacceptable will be accepted or pass the demo test.
2. The producers risk β, which is the risk that software that is acceptable will be rejected or fail the demo test.
3. The discrimination ratio γ, which represents the ratio in which the objective is met (think of it as the width of the area between the accept and reject lines in Fig. 6.1).

Once these parameters are determined, the graph shown in Figure 6.1 must be drawn by solving for two equations for a line. The two lines will always be parallel. In general, the equation of a line is $y = mx + a$.

The line between reject and continue in terms of the x axis, which will either be time (tests 2 and 3) or number of test inputs (test 4), is given by

Cumulative Number of Errors Found During Test

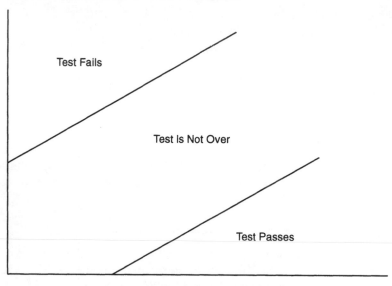

Test Fails

Test Is Not Over

Test Passes

Normalized Testing Time or Test Inputs

Figure 6.1   Reliability demonstration testing.

$$X = \frac{[\ln(1 - \alpha)/\beta] - Y \ln \gamma}{1 - \gamma}$$

The line between accept and continue in terms of the *x* axis, which will either be time (tests 2 and 3) or number of test inputs (test 4), is given by

$$X = \frac{[\ln \alpha/(1 - \beta)] - Y \ln \gamma}{1 - \gamma}$$

Solve for two points for each line and draw the lines. The last thing that must be done before beginning testing is to normalize the *x* axis for the reliability objective. You may do this by multiplying all of the points on the *x* axis by the failure rate objective or by multiplying all of the real *x* values that are collected during the test by the failure rate objective.

From the time the test begins you must plot each failure from 1, 2, . . . , *n* versus either time or number of test cases implemented. One of five events will occur:

1. If there are no failures, then when the number of test cases or testing time is equal to the value that intersects the x axis and the accept line, the test is over and the software has passed.
2. If the plot of failures versus test time or test inputs enters the reject region, then the test is over and the software has failed the reliability demo test.
3. If the plot of failures versus test time or test inputs enters the accept region, then the test is over and the software is accepted.
4. If the software reaches a state where maintenance is required in order for the software to continue with the test, the test is over and the software is rejected.
5. If none of the preceding four events occur, then the test is to continue until one of these events does occur.

You may ask how random test cases described in test 5 could be developed and then randomly input. This type of test will occur after all the other testing has been completed. Therefore, there should at this point be test cases and test procedures developed that validate the requirements of the software, the algorithms, and the structure. A method of selecting these test cases randomly and inputting them is proposed as follows.

It is important for test cases to be random in order to eliminate any bias, even unintentional, to select test cases that will either pass or fail. It is also important, however, that the software as a whole be adequately represented by the test cases so that the software is not rejected when it is actually acceptable and not accepted when it is actually not acceptable.

Selecting test cases that meet both of these objectives may be accomplished via blocking. Blocking as it pertains to software would be dividing up the software system into some number of major parts (these could be each of the major subprograms) and selecting random test cases from each of the major parts. This allows for randomness in selection of the test cases and also allows for the software code to be represented as completely as possible.

6.5   RANDOMNESS OF SOFTWARE FAULTS

The random variables with respect to software are the time of the next software failure and the location of the next software error. These are random variables because they are completely unknown. If these two items were not random variables, then there would be little need for the reliability models discussed in Chapter 8. A random process is set of random variables. Not only do we not know precisely when or where the next fault will occur, we do not know about any faults subsequent to the next one.

Even if you know enough about your software to know where the biggest problem areas are and to predict that the next error will probably be in some portion or function of the code, the next fault is still a random variable because you will not know precisely when or where the fault will manifest itself. If you knew this, then the error would no longer be an undetected error, it would be a fault. For example, if you perform a code walkthrough and find an error, then it is immediately no longer the next fault to be detected.

6.6   DISTRIBUTION OF SOFTWARE FAULTS

Exponential Distribution

If the errors are distributed exponentially, then the reliability may be expressed as

$$R(t) = e^{-at}$$

An exponential distribution with respect to software indicates a failure rate that is constant over time and a finite number of estimated inherent errors in the software.

Weibull Distribution

If software errors are distributed in a Weibull distribution, then the reliability of the software may be expressed as

$$R(t) = e^{-at^b}$$

The failure rate may or may not be constant over time.

Rayleigh Distribution

The Rayleigh distribution is a derivative of the Weibull distribution with the value of b defined as 2. If software errors are distributed in a Rayleigh distribution, then the reliability of the software may be expressed as

$$R(t) = e^{-at^2}$$

The failure rate is not constant over time.

Logarithmic Distribution

If the software errors are distributed logarithmically, then an infinite number of inherent software errors is assumed and the failure rate versus time is not constant. The logarithmic distribution assumes that bugs (such as the obvious ones or more frequently executed ones) are found first and that the rate of errors detected eventually levels off.

Nonhomogeneous Distribution

This is random process with a probability distribution that is variable. In software terms this means that software errors occur in batches. This has been found to be representative of software during the initial phases of development due to testing intensity.

Homogeneous Distribution

This is the converse of a nonhomogeneous distribution. It has been found to occur more often when the software has reached a stable state such as during operation.

6.7 SOFTWARE RELIABILITY PARAMETERS

Reliability is equal to

$$R(t) = e^{-[\int z(x)\, dx]}$$

where $z(x)$ is the hazard rate or conditional failure rate assuming no failures or faults occurring during the time interval.

Software mean time to failure (MTTF) is the time to the next software failure:

$$MTTF = \int R(x)\, dx$$

Cumulative number of software failures or faults is the total or cumulative number of software failures or faults that have occurred until some point in time, CED(t).

Software failure or fault intensity is the rate of change of cumulative faults or detected errors, CED(t)/t; see Figure 6.2.

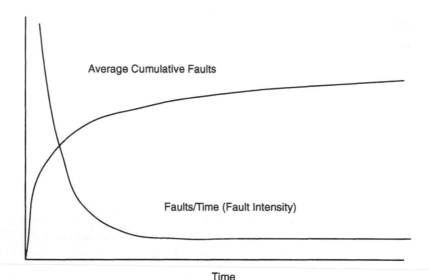

Figure 6.2   Software cumulative faults and fault intensity.

Reliability increases while the faults per time decrease. The average cumulative number of faults also increases as faults per time decrease; see Figure 6.3.

Cumulative number of software errors corrected is the total or cumulative number of software errors that have been corrected up until some point in time such that those corrections have been released to the end user, EC(t).

Mean software repair time is the average time to fix an error and test and verify the fix. This does not include any administrative time. It does include, however, the isolation of the source of the fault as well as the time to verify that the maintenance action has eliminated the fault and has not introduced any new faults.

Software mean turnaround time is the average time between a problem being reported and the problem being completely repaired at the development organization. This does not include any hold time due to a low-priority error.

Mean software release is the average time between software releases.

Time may be measured one of three ways. The first way is to measure CPU time. This basis of time is used in order to normalize the usage of the software over calendar time. The second way is to use operational

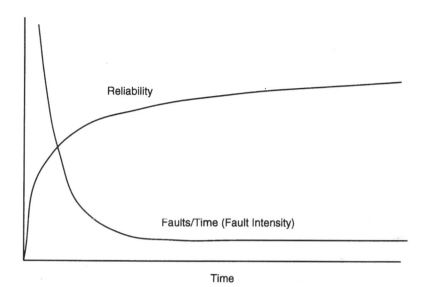

Figure 6.3 Software reliability and fault intensity.

time. This is the total time in which the software is being used. The third basis of time is calendar time. This assumes 24 hours a day, 7 days a week of testing or usage time. This author has found that operational time is practical and reflects the intensity of testing better than calendar time.

SUMMARY

This chapter provides the following information:

1. The basic definitions and types of software errors, including (a) coding errors, (b) requirements errors, and (c) external errors.
2. The types of software testing, including (a) tests performed over the life cycle, such as unit, integration, aceptance, and regression; (b) tests performed to verify specific results, which include algorithm, black box, white box, configuration, security, load and performance, and recovery; (c) software reliability testing, including a system reliability demonstration test, a software reliability demonstration test based on testing time, a software reliability dem-

onstration test based on test inputs, a beta test, and a reliability test based on results of the other tests described in (b); and (d) software reliability parameters including MTTF, failure rate, mean software repair time, mean turnaround time, mean software release time, and other parameters.

REFERENCE

Musa, J., Iannino, A., and Okumuto, K. *Software Reliability Measurement, Prediction, Application*, McGraw-Hill, New York, 1987.

PART II

Measuring Software Reliability

CHAPTER 7

Software Reliability Data Collection

Before any software reliability models can be successfully implemented in a real development environment, a scheme must be in place that allows for whatever inputs are used by the model(s) to be collected, organized, and analyzed. An effective data collection process is practical in that the amount and types of data are relatively simple to collect during development and test or at whatever phase of the life cycle the model or metric dictates the inputs are to be collected.

The data collection process is the most critical prerequisite to measuring software reliability. The effectiveness of any reliability measurement will be directly related to the effectiveness of collecting the data necessary for measurement. The three types of data that must be collected are (1) error data, (2) process data, and (3) product data.

There are many metrics associated with each of the three types of data to be collected. It is not advisable to begin implementing all of the metrics. First determine which ones should be used in your particular project or organization. Then determine where some potential problem areas are in your process and product. Begin to choose the metrics that may provide information in that problem area. Some of the metrics should be used all of the time, and they are indicated as such as they are discussed.

If there is no formal data collection process in place in your organization or in your vendor's organization, then one must be created. This chapter will show how to do exactly that, as well as how to improve an existing data collection process or modify an existing process for reliability measurement.

The data collection process must include a problem-reporting mechanism and may include a software configuration management system and possibly automated tools. The data collection process also includes collecting product and process data over and above problem report data. Collecting and measuring error data, product data, and process data will be discussed in this chapter. Configuration management and automated tools are discussed in Chapter 12.

7.1   COLLECTING AND MEASURING ERROR DATA VIA THE PROBLEM-REPORTING PROCESS

There are two objectives for an error-reporting process. The first is to report the right information needed for measuring the impact of the errors, and the second is to report it as efficiently as possible so that the resulting measurement may have impact on the development process and product.

The error- or problem-reporting process usually includes a problem report sheet, and an information flow process between each of the individuals and organizations responsible for modifying the software. A sample problem-reporting sheet is shown in Figure 7.1. The responsibility for collecting the data may be divided by various organizations, such as testing, quality assurance, reliability engineering, software development, systems engineering, etc. An organization flow for data collection is suggested in Figure 7.2.

The problem report should have three parts: (1) the error detection section, (2) the error correction section, and (3) the error correction verification section.

7.1.1   The Error Detection Information

Error detection information is generally filled out by the testing personnel. These personnel may be the person who developed the software,

Program area: _____ Identifier: _____
Date reported: / / Found by: _____ Version: _____
Status: _____ Open, Fixed, Review, Closed, No action
If no action: _____ Due to:

                    A. Duplicate
                    B. Unable to reproduce
                    C. Not a problem
                    D. New feature
                    E. Problem is obsolete

Bug severity:_____ 1 = High, 2 = Moderate, 3 = Low
Steps to reproduce error:

_____

_____
_____

Workaround:

_____
_____

Date corrected: / / Corrected by: _____ Version: _____
Time to fix (including isolation and checkout): _____
Action taken due to: _____ A. Previous maintenance

                    B. Change in requirements
                    C. New requirement
                    D. Unclear requirement
                    E. Incomplete requirement
                    F. Change in software environment
                    G. Change in hardware environment
                    H. Code/logic (not due to above)
                    I. Implemented enhancement
                    J. Other

Functions modified:

_____

_____
_____

Files modified:

_____
_____

Date verified: / / Verified by: _____ Version: _____
If not verified, describe reason:

_____
_____

Figure 7.1 Sample software trouble-reporting sheet.

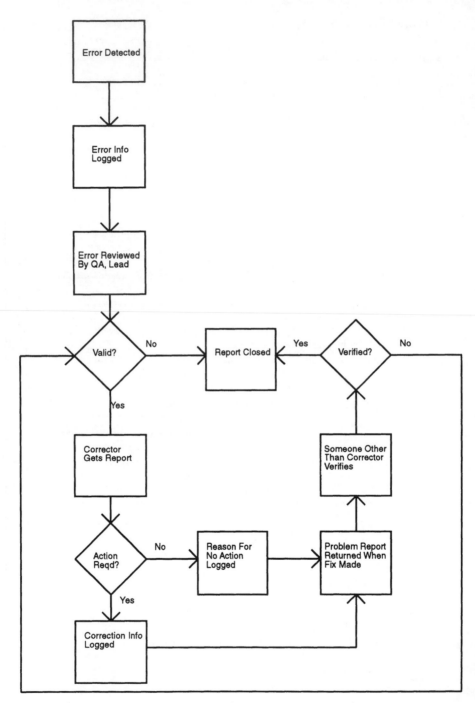

Figure 7.2   Flow chart of a problem-reporting process.

another developer, a completely independent testing person from outside of the organization, an independent tester from within the organization, a customer, or any person using the software who detects an error or anomaly in the software.

The detector as described above is responsible for recording the date the error was detected and a description of it as soon as possible after it was detected. If it is possible, the time of day may also be recorded. In order to expedite the correction of the problem, an accurate description of it should be given. This would include the sequence of events leading up to the problem, the data in memory when the problem occurred (if known by the user), the function being performed, and anything else that could be relevant. The author's experience is that this kind of information is in many cases not recorded as accurately as it could be.

Once the problem is recorded, the criticality, priority, and problem number are assigned by either a quality assurance person or a lead software engineer. The problem is usually reviewed by a review board or by the lead software engineer, and it is determined whether or not the problem is truly an error that must be corrected or whether the problem is rejected for reasons to be discussed shortly.

If the report does indicate a problem that must be fixed, it will be prioritized by its criticality and the estimated time required to fix it. Refer to Chapter 6 for instructions on determining the criticality of the error. The report is numbered sequentially and uniquely so that it can later be traced. The number may also be assigned so that it distinguishes where the problem was found functionally and who found it. For example, the first letter in the report number may indicate the group that found the problem, and the second letter may indicate the function of the software where the problem seems to be located.

7.1.2   Error Correction Information

The lead software engineer will then route the problem report to the person who is responsible for correcting it. This person may or may not be the same person who originally designed or coded the function. This depends on how the organization is structured and the personnel turnover within the organization.

The corrector isolates the problem, modifies the code, and then tests it to ensure that the change made adequately addresses the problem reported. One thing that the corrector should also do, but many times does not do, is test the change to make sure that it does not have an undesired effect on a software function that currently does work as required. The time that it takes to do all of this is the repair time. Do not be surprised to see this time stated in terms of days as opposed to hours, because the isolation and test time may far outweigh the time it took to make the change itself. The corrector records this time as well as the date the problem was finally corrected and possibly the time of day it was corrected. The corrector will also indicate the reason for the problem and the action taken to fix it. There are at least 10 possible reasons for the maintenance action:

1. Requirements Change

The corrector will indicate a requirements change as the reason for the maintenance action if the set of requirements originally used for developing the function containing the error was changed since the module was coded, and if the code would have been correct if the previous requirements were still in effect. This type of maintenance action is common on many software programs. Requirements may change because of customer needs or competition, particularly for commercial software.

2. New Requirement

The corrector will indicate a new requirement as the reason for the maintenance action if the set of requirements originally used for developing the function containing the error was changed to include a new requirement since the time when the function was coded. As with the maintenance action already described, this is also common owing to changing customer needs or changing interface requirements.

3. Misinterpretation of Requirements

The corrector will indicate this as the reason for the maintenance action if the person who coded the function misinterpreted the meaning of the stated requirements. In this case the requirements were not changed and were complete; however, the person designing or coding understood the requirements differently than expected. This will happen often if the software person does not have line-of-business experience in whatever application is being developed. For example, if the software is a financial banking application and the software engineer who designed or coded the software has never worked in a bank, then it is likely that he or she may at some time misinterpret the requirements.

4. Ambiguous Requirements

The corrector will indicate ambiguous requirements as the reason for a maintenance action when the stated requirements for which the function containing the error described by the problem report were not stated clearly enough for the person designing and coding to adequately do so. This could also include the case when the requirements were written, assuming that the developer understood certain unstated requirements. This is a very common reason for maintenance action, particularly when the end user and the software development team have not spent adequate time reviewing the requirements together to clear up any unstated assumptions. This reason for maintenance action differs from the one described earlier because the requirements are not defined properly. In some cases prototyping can reduce these types of software errors.

5. Previous Maintenance Action

The corrector will indicate a previous maintenance action as the cause of the software error when the error he or she corrected was not inherent in the software and was caused by an unexpected and undesired effect due to another change to the software made previously to this change. The number of errors due to previous maintenance may be surprisingly high. This author has seen it as high as four for every ten maintenance actions. These errors are also called regenerated errors. They are due primarily to a lack of sufficient check-out by persons correcting errors, caused by lack of resources or systematic methodologies.

6. Coding or Logic Error

The corrector will identify coding or logic error as the reason for a maintenance action when the error was due solely to one of the following:

  a. An incorrect implementation of an algorithm
  b. Lack of initialization of variables
  c. Improper initialization of variables
  d. Coding errors not found until run time or integration
  e. Improper parameter passing
  f. Improper use of language and operating system
  g. Any other error not due to a requirements, design, or maintenance defect.

7. *Performance Error*

The corrector will indicate a performance error as the source of a maintenance action when a change is necessary to improve the efficiency, response time, and resource usage. This improvement must be necessary to meet the stated requirements; otherwise it may be considered an enhancement.

8. *Change in Hardware Environment Error*

The corrector will indicate a change in environment error when the maintenance action was due solely to a change in the hardware configuration and interfaces.

9. *Change in Software Environment Error*

The corrector will identify a change in software environment error as the reason for a maintenance action when external software, such as the operating system, development environment, or any other external software interface is modified and is the sole reason for the error.

10. *Incomplete and Inadequate Design*

The corrector will identify design as the reason for maintenance action when it is obvious that the code is not the problem but the design approach is. If the software was not designed in a structured approach and an error is detected or a change necessitated because of it, then this is the reason for maintenance action.

It is also possible that the corrector may make no software change at all. There are seven reasons why this may occur. Some of these reasons may be found before the corrector is ever given the responsibility for fixing the software problem and rejected by the lead software engineer or quality assurance engineer.

11. *Duplicate Error*

The problem is rejected because it has already been previously detected.

12. *Anomaly Is Not an Error*

The problem detected and documented on the problem report is not an error. This could be due to the detector not understanding the purpose of the software or scope of the requirements.

13.   Enhancement or New Feature

The problem detected is not within the scope of the requirements; however, it is a good idea and may possibly be considered at a later point in time. This could include some performance changes or cosmetic changes not specifically required.

14.   Anomaly Cannot Be Duplicated

The problem detected cannot be duplicated by the corrector; therefore the problem cannot be isolated and fixed. This may happen if the detector is testing on a different version of software than the corrector or if the problem was due to insufficient memory resources. The information should be kept, however, so that if at some time more information is known, then the problem may be fixed.

15.   Hold

The problem may be put on hold if it is not as critical as other problems that need to be addressed first, if it would require an extensive redesign that may not be worth the resources it would take to implement, or if insufficient information is known about the problem.

16.   Documentation Error

If the anomaly was due to incorrect instructions contained in the operator's or user's manual and those incorrect instructions caused an error, then the problem is a documentation error and the software is not modified.

17.   Error Is Too Impractical to Fix

If the error is detected at the point in the development where a major design change would be necessary to implement it, it could be rejected for that reason if the necessity for fixing it is outweighed by the cost to do so.

The 17 reasons for maintenance actions described above need to be tracked carefully for two reasons. First, the models and metrics will require that problem reports that are not determined to be errors not be counted as such. Second, the distribution of these types of errors is an important piece of information necessary for improving the reliability of the software.

In order to use any of the models, counting the total number of problem reports opened is not sufficient—each one must be tracked. Any problem report that has a resulting maintenance action described in 11, 12, 13, 14, and 16 cannot be considered as a software error because there is no resulting change made to the software. Type 17 can be considered to be an error even though it may never be fixed.

You may ask whether problems due to change in software requirements, addition of software requirements, change in hardware environment, or change in software environment are really "software" errors, since the source of the error was not a problem in the original software design. This is a debatable issue. The fact is that these types of problems are very often a big part of the software design process. On the one hand, we could model only the software code and design errors and discard these four types of problems; however, we would not be modeling the true development environment, nor would we be accurately reflecting the development (hardware and software) system as a whole. On the other hand, by lumping these types of problems with the other true software errors, we would not be modeling the software environment by itself as accurately. There is a solution to this delemma.

First, we can and should include these types of problems when modeling the software reliability if we are truly interested in modeling the real-life development process. However, we should track the distribution of all 10 types of problems requiring maintenance action so that it is obvious where the potential problem areas lie, not only within the software development organization but within the entire development process.

This is done by tracking the cumulative numbers of each problem type discovered over the same period of time. A pie or Pareto chart does an excellent job of representing this distribution. This distribution can now be used in conjunction with the other models and metrics as a comprehensive means of measuring the overall software development process. Development personnel will probably gain the most from the results of the distribution data because they may use it to identify problem areas and areas for improvement. A chart of data collected by the author is shown later in this chapter in the case studies section.

If the distribution chart shows that a relatively large number of errors are from a change in software requirements, this indicates a problem with the process itself and not necessarily the people who are designing and coding the software. If a large number of errors are from new requirements, this indicates the same type of situation described earlier, only it is probably due to insufficient time spent in the concept and requirements phase. It probably also indicates a strong influence from one or more customers.

If a large portion of errors are due to misinterpreting requirements, then line-of-business training may need to be made available so that the software persons have a clearer understanding of the end-user needs. If there are many errors due to ambiguous requirements, then this indicates a need for more informal and formal reviews during the requirements and design phase in order to clarify the requirements document.

If there is a relatively large number of errors due to logic and code errors, then this probably indicates inexperience on behalf of the coders. If you track the relative proportion of these errors over a substantial period of time, assuming an insignificant turnover of personnel, this distribution should decrease as experience increases. In-house training may also be needed for improvement.

If many of the errors are due to previous maintenance action, then this indicates a lack of check-out during the correcting process. This probably also indicates that there may not be a systematic method for ensuring that a change to fix one error will not cause another error. McCabe's structured maintenance is one methodology that could prevent these errors; see Chapter 9 for more information. A high number of these errors could also be due to no check-out at all if the corrector is attempting to turn around the problem report too quickly.

If a large number of maintenance actions are due to improving performance to meet the requirements, this indicates a possible lack of a structured design or understanding of the available resources which are available. Familiarity with the resource limits of the hardware may be obtained through experience or training.

A relatively large number of maintenance actions due to a change in hardware environment indicates a problem with the system process and requirements. To reduce these errors would require making improvements at a system (hardware and software) level. As most software developers know, this is not always the easiest task to accomplish. Total quality management training for an entire organization may be one solution.

A large number of errors caused by a change in external software may be due to one of two reasons. If the changes are due to external software that is developed within the organization or by a subcontractor, then these errors will require the solution already described for a change in hardware environment. However, if the software is externally purchased software such as operating systems, these types of errors may be unavoidable.

Keeping track of the reasons for maintenance actions will provide software management with a valuable process indicator and tool for improvement. If the intention is to improve the reliability of the software, then it is not enough to simply count the number of errors that occur over some period of time. The source of these errors must also be known.

In addition to the reason for the maintenance action, the corrector must also log what module(s) were affected by the change and the time it took to isolate, fix, and check out the maintenance action. The corrector should indicate how many and which module(s) was modified. The corrector must also log the date in which it was finally fixed and if possible the time of day. If no change was made to the software for one of the seven reasons discussed, then the corrector must indicate which reason and why.

One reason for logging the number of modules modified is so the severity of all of the error corrections may be measured. Some corrective actions may only be a change to one or two lines of code, while others may be a change to the large percentage of the existing modules. By tracking the number of modules changed by each corrective action, the maximum, minimum, and average number of modules changed per corrective action may be measured. This information may be very valuable in projecting manpower resources and costs for maintenance. The severity of the corrective actions is information that can be used in conjunction with the maximum, minimum, and average time to make a corrective action. Ideally, a distribution of different levels of severity based on number of modules changed for a corrective action should be used.

7.1.3   Error Correction Validation

Once the error is corrected, the corrector will turn the problem report over to the lead software engineer or quality assurance engineer so that it may be sent to an appropriate person who will verify that the problem described in the report was fixed appropriately. This person may have been the same one who initiated the report, or it may be an independent person. It cannot be, however, the same person who made the correction. The verifier should not only check to assure that the change was made properly, but if possible should check to assure that there are no unexpected and undesirable side effects of the change. If the verifier finds the change to be acceptable, then he or she will sign the problem report and date it. If the verifier does not find the change to be acceptable, then he or she will date it but return it back to the corrector. It may take more than one iteration before the verifier is willing to accept the change and sign off the report. At this point the problem report is now officially closed.

The problem-reporting system was described as being a manual process. This process can be automated and at many software development organizations it is at least partially automated. In order to automate this problem-reporting process the amount of computer space necessary for holding the problem information must be investigated. The security of the system must also be investigated. (It would be necessary to have each part of the problem report not accessible for writing to every user.) Each of the detectors, correctors, and verifiers needs to have easy access to the system. A mail system would be necessary to send the information to each detector, corrector, and verifier. A central system must be in place for the initial analysis of the problem report. A mechanism for tracking any supporting information such as printouts must be accounted for. In short, it must be determined if it is even necessary to have an automated problem-report system. The author has witnessed many situations where it was not; see Chapter 12 for more information on automating this process.

Whether or not the problem-reporting system is automated is probably not as important as the information collected. The reporting system should be as uncumbersome to the user as possible. There should be no "reliability" terms such as MTTF on the report itself. The persons most likely to be the detectors, correctors, and verifiers are generally not (almost never) from a reliability background. This author has experienced implementation of a problem report that was more than two full pages long and contained inputs for statistics most software engineers would never have heard of. Consequently, the problem report sheets were never filled out at all. The job of the software engineer is to develop the software as efficiently as possible, taking into account many design parameters, of which reliability is only one. A problem-reporting system that is too cumbersome will not allow them to do that. All of the information needed to calculate reliability may be obtained through normal information collected during the development process. Implementing a problem-reporting process that does not meet the discussed criteria may actually have a negative impact on the end reliability of the software, since more time is spent measuring than was spent on development itself.

Once the problem-report data collection begins, organize this data to obtain some useful information. Determine the error detection rate for each point in time in which an error was discovered. A graph of this error rate is advised because it is very useful. You will also need to determine the correction rate for every point in time in which a correction was made. This rate should also be graphed.

The cumulative number of errors and error rates for each error criticality should be tracked. You may choose to sort them by critical and noncritical or by the five categories discussed in Chapter 3. This is an extremely useful indicator, particularly when release time is approaching.

The total number of problem reports as well as the total number of errors described by the problem reports must be collected. Do not assume that there is exactly one software error for every problem report. One problem report may address several software errors.

The total number of errors corrected at any point in time must be collected. The time the error is corrected must be associated with it (this information comes from the problem report). The total number of errors verified as corrected must be tracked also. Track the cumulative number of errors verified as corrected, since the problem report is not officially closed until the error is verified as corrected.

7.2   PROCESS DATA TO BE COLLECTED

While data are being collected during the problem-reporting process, other data must also be collected that are process specific. Process data is extremely important in order to put the collected data into the proper perspective, and to use many of the reliability models available today.

One important data item that must be collected is the amount of time spent on a periodic basis developing, coding, testing, and maintaining the software.

Many of the reliability models are used during integration and systems testing as well as on field data. If the models are to be used during the testing phase, then it is necessary to track the time spent testing from the beginning of the phase until release to the customer. This is not as easy as it may sound, and there are different approaches to doing this.

Some authors use CPU time as the basis for time. The advantage to doing this is that it is a uniform measure that takes into account the fact that testing effort is not uniform during the phase. The disadvantage to using CPU time is that it does not account for much of the manual labor involved in reviewing, isolating problems, and coding. Calendar time is the easiest to collect (particularly if you assume 8 hours a day for 5 days a week as an example); however, it does not take into account the fact that some forms of testing are more efficient than others and that some people are more efficient at coding and testing than others. Operational time may also be used as a basis. This would be the total time in which the software was being used. As with calendar time, it still may not account for variations in testing efficiency. Operational time, however, may be weighted if it is known that during some period of time more or less testing was performed than normal. The basis for time must be determined *before* any metrics or models are used, regardless of which basis is chosen.

The average repair time or corrective action time should be calculated by summing each of the repair times on each problem report in which a maintenance action was performed. Divide this number by the total number of problem reports in which a maintenance action occurred. In addition to the average corrective action time, the maximum and minimum corrective action times as well as a distribution of action times should be calculated. The author has found that the average corrective action time in many cases has limited value in projecting future manpower requirements for maintenance.

The mean turnaround time is calculated by summing the time between when the problem report was detected until it was corrected (subtracting any hold time) and dividing by the total number of problem reports in which a maintenance action occurred. This measure is a process measure, because it reflects how the organization responds to detected errors.

The number of personnel performing each activity must be tracked. This includes the total number of personnel who design, code, test, and maintain. The number of people who maintain the software is of particular interest. The man-hours expended per unit time (month) must be tracked. Also, the man-hours expended in a particular activity such as repair time per function or requirement should be tracked. From this metric the cost of corrective action may be derived.

The percentage of time spent in each phase of the life cycle should be tracked. This includes the percentage of time spent in requirements analysis, top-level design, detailed design, coding, unit testing, integration and system testing, and maintenance. Also, the amount of resources spent in each phase should be tracked to determine potential areas for reducing costs.

The start date of the phase (integration testing) must be collected as well as the release date(s). Any internal release dates must also be tracked, as well as any significant milestones. Another important data item is the number of links or major recompiles during the testing and field phases.

The phase in which each error was generated as well as the phase in which each error was detected should be tracked. Also track the amount of man-hours spent fixing each error in each phase. This will indicate which types of errors are causing the most impact at which phase in development.

Another distribution chart that should be used is the phase of the life cycle in which the errors are introduced and a complementary chart indicating at which phase of the life cycle errors are detected. These two charts should be used in conjunction with each other in order to draw the correct conclusions on which phase or phases of the life cycle could use some improvement with respect to reliability.

For example, if you collected data on the life-cycle phase in which errors were detected and found that the majority were during unit testing, your first reaction might be that more effort needs to be expended during the phases that precede or even include the unit testing phase. However, if you had data that illustrated that most of the errors were introduced during the unit test phase, then the original assumption would be invalid.

Historical data may be very valuable. All of the data that we have described so far make excellent historical data. If there is a program previously developed that is similar to the current program being developed, then you may want to use the mean time to failure or failure rate of the software previously developed as a starting point for this program. You can only do this if you consistently track data from program to program. You may also keep historical data on the reliability growth rate discussed in Chapter 8. See the fourth case study at the end of Chapter 8 for an example.

Track the testing time spent per function and the number of errors per function or module to determine some problem areas.

Modules that have had a relatively large amount of testing time spent on them may continue to be a problem in the future due to a possible major design flaw. The author collected data on one module of a software program that experienced testing time that far outweighed the average testing time for every other module. It was found that the error rate on this module alone increased over time, even though its testing time was also increased over time. The module was later rewritten and decomposed into three smaller modules.

One extremely important process metric is the amount of time spent in walkthroughs that were successful and productive in preventing or eliminating design or code errors. It is not enough to simply measure how much or how many walkthroughs were conducted. The degree to which those walkthroughs were successful must also be measured.

The number of action items taken during a walkthrough that were acted upon within some interval of time can be measured, as well as the percentage of action items that were acted upon at all as a result of the walkthrough. This will measure the effectiveness of the walkthrough process. If it is possible, you may want to measure how many detected errors could have been avoided if a walkthrough had been performed during either design or coding. You may want to implement these metrics if you have no inspection or walkthrough process at all, or if you suspect that your inspection process is not effective.

The percentage of maintenance actions that are due solely to rework should be tracked, if there is reason to believe that rework is costing your organization time and resources.

The percentage of errors corrected in some range of times such as 1, 4, 8, or 12 hours, as well as the mean, median, maximum, and minimum corrective active time, should be tracked in order to assess maintenance schedules and turnaround times on corrective actions.

The corrective action time must be defined consistently. Ideally, any isolation time should be included, as well as the actual time it took to repair the code. Also note that this corrective action time may not have complete meaning unless a turnaround time is also measured. The average turnaround time is the average total time between detecting a bug and releasing the fix back to the end user. You may encounter very low corrective action times but have a high turnaround time due to other organization factors.

Another type of process data is testing coverage. The degree to which the code is effectively and efficiently verified reflects the software development process. Determine testing coverage by measuring the percentage of functions that were completely unit tested according to a standard set of unit testing procedures (see Chapter 9), and the percentage of functions that were completely system tested for conformance to requirements (see Chapter 9).

7.3   PRODUCT DATA TO BE COLLECTED
AND MEASURED

Product data is data specific to the product being developed with respect to its size, functionality, complexity, and other characteristics that are specific to a particular product. One product data item that may be necessary to collect, depending on which models or metrics are implemented, is an executable line of code estimate. If it is known that the number of executable lines of code varies significantly during development, then it will be necessary to estimate the number periodically.

There are tools available to count lines of code, or a program may be written fairly easily to do this. If the number does not very significantly, then it may only be necessary to estimate this number once or twice (at the beginning and end of the phase). At one time, it was commonly felt that the lines of code estimate was an acceptable measure for software productivity, quality and reliability. In recent times, however, the lines-of-code estimate has have proven to be an inaccurate and irrelevant measure of software for many reasons. First, the lines-of-code estimate will vary from language to language. It will also vary from experienced to inexperienced persons. Experienced software persons are more likely to have less lines of code, and therefore their errors per line of code estimate will be pessimistic, because there will be fewer lines of code. Lines-of-code estimates measure the volume and not necessarily the quality or reliability of the software. The author does not recommend using lines of executable code as any basis for measure other than for measuring software volume.

If reusable code is being used, you should track the number of errors and amount of man-hours spent fixing the reusable code. This will indicate whether reusable code was reused appropriately or not.

Other product metrics are the total number of functions traceable to a specification, the total number of functions, the number of calling routines, and the total number of data references.

One important metric is the cyclomatic complexity per module or function. This is the structural complexity of each module of the software (see Chapter 9 for more information). The complexity count of each module is relatively simple to compute and collect with the appropriate tools implemented. It is generally believed that modules that are more complex than others may be more error-prone than others because they are less testable and less maintainable than less complex modules. It may be desired to track the number of errors per module or per subcomponent (group of modules) to determine the relationship between complexity and errors.

The Case Studies section of this chapter is a summary of complexity and error count data collected on a real software development program. The program consisted of 800 executable modules and the data shown were collected over an 8-month period of time.

One product metric is the percentage of functions or code that is documented properly according to some set of documentation standards (see Chapter 9). This metric may be useful if a lack of maintainability of the software seems to be a source of rework or errors.

Other product metrics are the percentage of units that have one entrance and one exit, the percentage of units functionally independent of other units, and the percentage of units that have locally as opposed to globally defined variables. These metrics indicate how flexible, maintainable, and reliability the software is, based on design principles.

One last product metric that should be tracked is the errors per location of source code. This metric will indicate which areas of the code are more error-prone.

7.4 CASE STUDIES

Data collected from four different types of software development programs are presented in this section. The four types of programs were (1) financial software, (2) military software, (3) insurance software, and (4) engineering software.

7.4.1 Case Study 1

This case study involved financial software that was developed entirely in PASCAL and was approximately 200,000 lines of executable code. The software was composed of three functional subprograms, which were each developed under three separate development managers. The development environment was semidetached in that the software engineers had various levels of experience. Before the software reached the coding phase, a process was put in place and agreed upon by development and quality assurance.

The error tracking process was to be performed manually by logging the error detection, correction, and verification information on paper. However, the data itself were later entered into a spreadsheet and analyzed by using a DBMS system. The information tracked was similar to that described in Figure 7.1.

The following metrics were used for the results and the improvements made during integration and systems testing:

1. Number of errors detected over testing time
2. Number of errors corrected over testing time
3. Number of errors verified as correct over testing time
4. Number of critical errors detected, corrected, and verified as correct over testing time
5. Number of moderate errors detected, corrected, and verified as correct over testing time
6. Number of negligible errors detected, corrected, and verified as correct over testing time
7. Number of documentation errors detected, corrected, and verified over testing time
8. All error data contained in Figure 7.1
9. Number of errors detected, corrected, and verified as correct per area of source code

The most interesting results of the metrics are illustrated in Figure 7.3 and 7.4. In Figure 7.3 are shown

A: Number of errors due to changing requirements
B: Number of errors due to design
C: Number of errors due to new requirements
D: Number of errors due to logic and coding
E: Number of errors due to misinterpreted requirements
F: Number of errors due to previous maintenance

Figure 7.3 shows that 26% of all errors detected were due to changing requirements, 25% to incomplete and inadequate design methodologies, 18% to new requirements, 9% to logic and coding, 4% to misinterpreted requirements, and 18% to previous maintenance actions. In summary, 73% of all errors were due to either requirements or design.

Figure 7.4 shows that the cumulative number of errors detected over time continued to increase and did not level off. Figure 7.5 shows that the cumulative number of critical errors over time not only did not level off but exhibited a peak toward the end of the testing period.

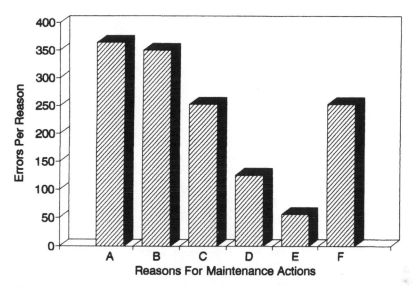

Figure 7.3 Reasons for maintenance actions versus number of errors.

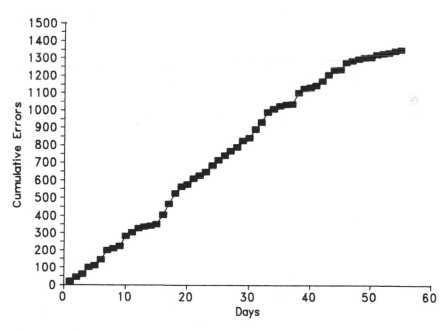

Figure 7.4 Cumulative errors versus days.

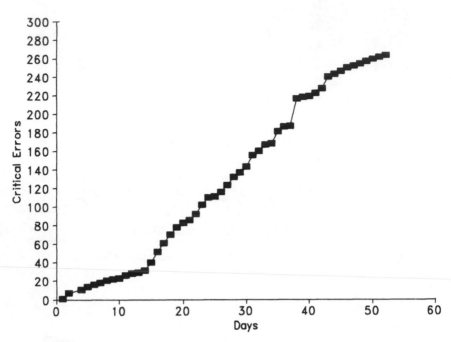

Figure 7.5 Critical errors versus days.

The combination of these two metrics indicates a software development process that is out of control. The sources of the errors indicate that the organization was attempting to shoot a moving requirements target since 48% of the errors were due solely to requirements. The fact that 25% were due to design indicates a lack of a systematic process. Indeed, this was the case.

The organization was attempting to compete with another product being developed by another corporation. The requirements of the product were never agreed upon and were continually changed as the competitor's product changed. One component of the software was developed from the bottom up as opposed to from the top down. This component was eventually redesigned and rewritten.

The continual change in requirements was the major reason why the error rate continued to increase as opposed to decrease over time. Another reason was that the rate of introducing errors due solely to maintenance was found to be four for every ten errors corrected. This regeneration rate was determined from the problem-reporting data collected.

This development project experienced three major problems during the life cycle, which eventually resulted in loss of revenue and a complete redesign of the entire system. The most critical problem was the inability to freeze the software requirements to stabilize the development process. The second most critical problem was the lack of a systematic process, which allowed an incomplete design to go unnoticed and unchecked until the integration testing phase. Effective walkthroughs and inspections would have most likely prevented this from happening. The third most critical problem was due to the high rate of introducing errors during maintenance on other errors. This indicates a lack of structured maintenance procedures as well as a lack of structured design procedures.

Unfortunately, the only metrics that were made visible to management during the testing process were the error detection rate and the errors detected per development person. This is an example of a misuse of metrics. The software engineers were evaluated based on the number of errors detected in the source code that they developed. Consequently, the developers did not disclose any errors that they knew about in their software. The errors were found too late in the development cycle to correct. In actuality, a small percentage (27%) of the total errors detected was directly attributed to the software engineers themselves. The other 73% were attributed to the entire development process.

7.4.2 Case Study 2

This case study involves real-time software that was developed almost entirely in FORTRAN and was approximately 300,000 lines of code. The software was composed of seven functional components and had approximately 800 modules. The development environment was very large and detached. There were numerous hardware interface requirements for the software, and the software requirements changed often. The problem-reporting system was for the most part manual. A problem-reporting scheme similar to that described previously was implemented.

The following metrics were used for the results and improvements made during the life cycle:

1. All problem-report data are as described in Figure 7.1
2. Cumulative number of errors detected, corrected, and verified over testing time

3. Cumulative number of critical errors detected, corrected, and verified over testing time.
4. Cumulative number of moderate errors detected, corrected, and verified over testing time.
5. Cumulative number of negligible errors detected, corrected, and verified over testing time.
6. Total and average corrective action time.
7. It was known that every module in the program had exactly one entrance and exit.
8. The cyclomatic complexity of every module was known.
9. With the exception of two modules, every module was known to perform exactly one function.
10. The testing time per component and per module was known.
11. The number of errors detected, corrected, and verified as correct per module and per component was known.

The most interesting results of these metrics is shown in Figures 7.6, 7.7, 7.8, and 7.9. In Figure 7.6 the x axis represents:

A: Number of errors due to logic or code
B: Number of errors due to ambiguous requirements
C: Number of errors due to changing requirements
D: Number of errors due to new features
E: Number of errors due to documentation

It was found that the errors detected were due mostly to logic/code misinterpretation of requirements, changing requirements, and new features. Unfortunately, even though these metrics were collected, they were never made visible until very near the release date. It was erroneously assumed that the errors were due 100% to coding and logic. Efforts were made to improve the coding process, when it was actually the analysis and design process that was responsible for most of the errors.

Figure 7.7 shows the severity of each maintenance action as described:

A: Action required change to 1 module
B: Action required change to 2 modules
C: Action required change to 3–4 modules
D: Action required change to 5–6 modules
E: Action required change to 7–8 modules

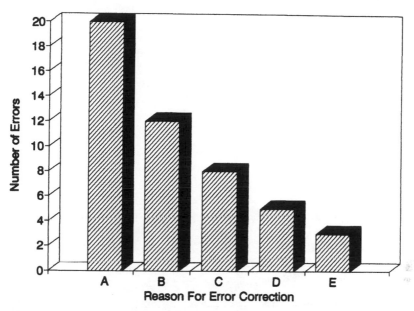

Figure 7.6   Reason for error correction.

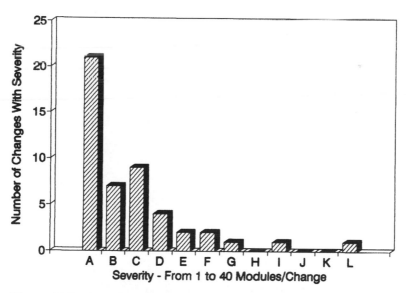

Figure 7.7   Severity of error corrections: number of modules modified per change.

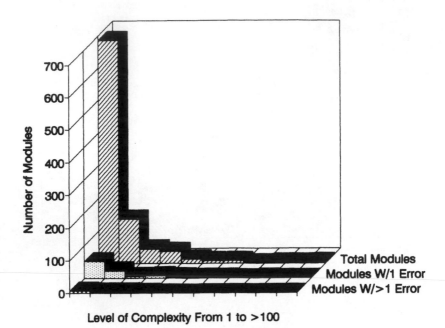

Figure 7.8   Complexity and errors per module.

  F: Action required change to 9–10 modules
  G: Action required change to 11–15 modules
  H: Action required change to 16–20 modules
   I: Action required change to 21–25 modules
  J: Action required change to 26–30 modules
  K: Action required change to 31–35 modules
  L: Action required change to 36–40 modules

Half of the maintenance actions required change to only one module, and the other half required change to from 2 to 40 modules. This was an indication that at least some of the software was probably not designed to be modular.

Figure 7.8 shows the number of modules with some level of complexity and the number of errors found in the modules. The x axis shows the modules with:

  A: Complexity ≤ 10.
  B: Complexity > 10 and < 20

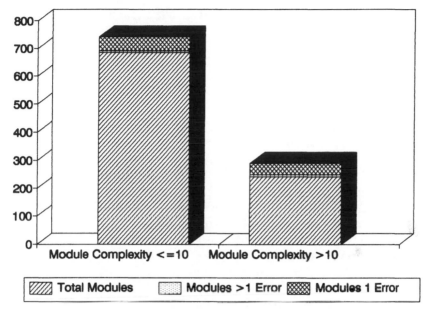

Figure 7.9 Relationship of errors to complexity.

    C: Complexity > 20 and ≤ 30
    D: Complexity > 30 and ≤ 40
    E: Complexity > 40 and ≤ 50
    F: Complexity > 50 and ≤ 60
    G: Complexity > 60 and ≤ 70
    H: Complexity > 70 and ≤ 80
    I: Complexity > 80 and ≤ 90
    J: Complexity > 90

This graph was used to determine if there is a relationship between errors and complexity. According to this graph the complexity does not seem to have a relationship with modules that have more than one error detected in them. Nor does there seem to be a relationship with modules that have exactly one error. One interesting note is that the highest module complexity was 212 and that module had no errors detected in it. This particular graph does not show a relationship between complexity and errors; however, some additional information such as the usage factor of each module may show that some of the complex modules may be used less often.

Figure 7.9 shows the complexity information for modules that have a complexity less than or equal to 10 or greater than 10. This graph shows that there is a larger percentage of modules with more than two errors with a complexity greater than 10.

7.4.3   Case Study 3

This case involved insurance software that had approximately 100,000 lines of C executable code. There were five functional subprograms. The development organization was organic in that the developers worked very closely together and had very similar backgrounds. The problem-reporting process was similar to that in Figure 7.1 and was performed semimanually. The reports were generated on paper but later logged into a system that analyzed the problem-report data.

The following are the metrics used for results and improvements made for this case study:

1. Number of errors detected and corrected during systems testing. (There was no formal verification process.)
2. Number of critical errors detected and corrected during systems testing.
3. Number of negligible errors detected and corrected during systems testing.
4. Number of actions taken due to inspections and walkthroughs of design and code.
5. Problem-report data described in Figure 7.1.
6. Cost of error correction.

This case study is different from the previous two because of a very small and informal development group. There was direct contact with the customer; however, many of the requirements were defined informally. The software was designed from the top down. As each component was completed, the customer had the opportunity to review the partial system.

The sources of all errors detected once in beta test are illustrated in Figure 7.10. The errors were due to ambiguous requirements, changing requirements, and logic or code. Most of these errors can be attributed to the informal requirements analysis phase and the informal error-correction verification process.

Of the total errors detected, 31% were classified as critical and 69% were classified as negligible. Many of the negligible errors were due to

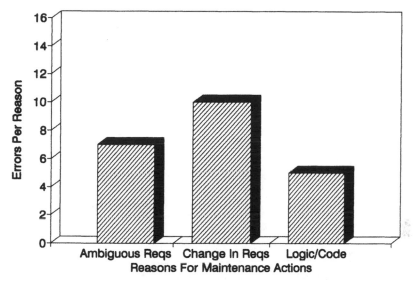

Figure 7.10 Reasons for maintenance actions versus number of errors.

the fact that the customer had absolutely no experience as a computer user and made many errors that were, for the most part, not avoidable by the software program.

Even though there was not a high number of error corrections, the time spent making each correction was found to be very high, 160 man-hours, because of the extent and severity of each change. There was also cost involved due to reconstruction of lost data.

The metrics were used to improve the process by requiring procedures for verification of error corrections and for regression testing. There were also formalized procedures put in place for defining new requirements, and for defining the performance criteria. Since the improvements were made, two moderate errors requiring only 4 hours of corrective action time were found during the next year.

7.4.4 Case Study 4

Metrics collected on the development of an engineering tool are presented as case study 4. This software was developed in C and is approximately 400,000 lines of executable code. It is mathematically intensive and is composed of 12 subprograms. There are 400 modules in the program. The problem-reporting information discussed earlier was collected while testing the software.

The following are the metrics used for the results and the improvement process implemented on this case study.

1. All problem-reporting data shown in Figure 7.1 were collected.
2. The cumulative errors detected, correct, and verified as correct over testing time.
3. The number of critical errors detected, corrected, and verified as correct over testing time.
4. The number of moderate errors detected, corrected, and verified as correct over testing time.
5. The number of negligible errors detected, corrected, and verified as correct over testing time.
6. The number of errors detected, corrected, and verified as correct per component of source code.
7. The number of modules modified per corrective action.

Figure 7.11 illustrates the distribution of error sources. This project experienced many new requirements as well as many errors due to design and coding and logic errors. Figure 7.11 shows:

A: Action due to previous maintenance
B: Action due to new requirements
C: Action due to changing requirements
D: Action due to ambiguous requirements
E: Action due to change in software environment
F: Action due to change in hardware environment
G: Action due to missing requirements
H: Action due to logic/code
 I: Action due to documentation
J: Action due to other causes

Figure 7.12 shows the errors found by location in source code. There were 12 primary functions of the software. Six of those were available in the first release, eight were available in the second release, and 10 in the third release. This graph shows that location 1 had almost consistently the most errors detected in that version. For locations 2–5, the relative number of errors does not appear to vary much from release to release. In the final release, one new function exhibited the highest number of

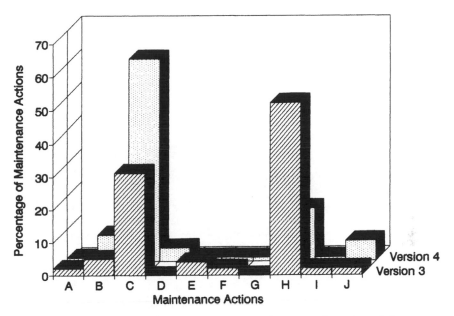

Figure 7.11 Reasons for maintenance actions, versions 3 and 4.

errors ever. It was found that the requirements for that new function continually changed even into the testing phase. This function was also extremely visible to the user and was used 100% of the time that the software was operational.

Figure 7.13 shows the criticality of each error detected in each version. In the first two versions, the errors were detected entirely by customers and were mostly rated as critical errors. In the last two versions, however, the errors were found by both the customers and the developers. It seems interesting that the errors seem to be fairly evenly divided as critical, moderate, and negligible. This chart illustrated an unexpected but interesting result in that the development team may not be aware of their customers priorities and needs. In any case, a chart similar to this one was used continually to determine how many errors required an immediate correction.

This software had been developed from the bottom up. New code was added to old code with no formal methodologies for design or test. It was found that unit testing did not exist at all, due to lack of tools and methodologies. The software was compiled and then tested as a system

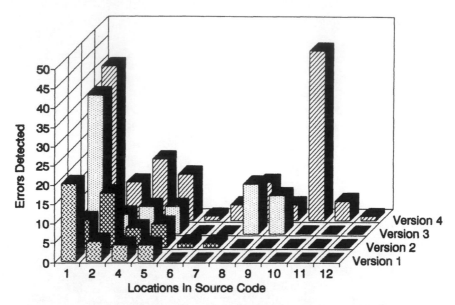

Figure 7.12 Number of errors detected versus location in source code.

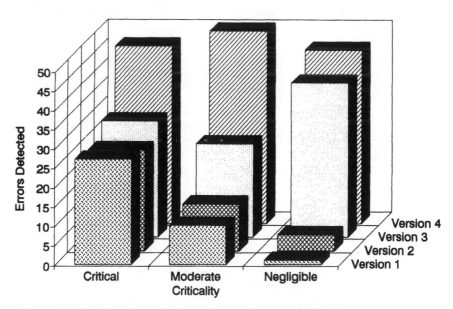

Figure 7.13 Number of errors detected versus criticality.

with no time allowed for testing from the developers point of view. Fortunately, there were effective procedures in place for coding, complexity, and documentation.

The results of the metrics were used to improve the design methodologies, to implement procedures for unit testing, and to establish a systematic process for developing software. Management was very aware of these results and was willing to make modifications to the development process in stages. The first stage was the implementation of unit testing. These procedures showed visible results in 6 months. Later, the software was delivered with no known errors in it.

SUMMARY

There are many, many metrics that may be implemented for various purposes during each phase of the life cycle. It is very important that what must be measured is determined before data collection begins. Data collection is expensive and will only have a payback if it is done effectively and efficiently. Determine initially what it is you want to know about your software process and then determine how to collect that data. The data must be collected in a consistent manner from that point on to reduce in the data variability that will make any software metric or model become less accurate or invalid.

In summary, collection of error data, process data, and product data is extremely important not only for measuring software reliability but also for improving it. Software reliability measures will only be as accurate as the data that are input into them. The less variance in the data, the more accurate and usable the model will be. A problem-reporting process as well as some tools for collecting the data will be necessary.

Tables 7.1, 7.2, and 7.3 summarize the error data metrics, process data metrics, and product data metrics.

Table 7.1   Summary of Software Error Metrics

Metric	Description
Problem reporting error data: (These data should be collected on all projects.) Date each error is detected Time each error is detected Description of how error was detected Area of program error was detected in Name of person detecting error Status of the error	Open, fixed, closed, review
Unique identifier!	Used to sort and identify types of errors.
Priority/severity	Indication of how urgent the error correction is.
Date error corrected Name of person correcting error Maintenance action taken Number of modules modified Names of modules modified Version control information Description of modification Time required to correct error Date verified as corrected Name of person verifying correction	
Cumulative errors detected	This metric should be used on every project to determine the error rate and reliability as well as a visual guide to the stability of the software. This curve of errors detected over time should eventually level off. Software engineers and managers should find this

Table 7.1   (Continued)

Metric	Description
	metric useful for improving development and projections.
Cumulative errors corrected	This metric is useful for determining how many known errors still require a corrective action. It is also useful for determining how responsive the correction process is.
Cumulative errors verified corrected	This metric is important because until an error is verified as being corrected, it cannot be assumed that it is. This is a count of all closed problems.
Cumulative severe errors detected	This metric is useful for every project to determine what percentage of known errors must be responded to immediately and to estimate reliability and project trends focusing on just the severe errors. These metrics can and should be used on all projects.
Error detection rate	This metric is used to indicate a trend. The rate should decrease as the software is used and tested; however, it may continue to increase if the requirements are changed or if corrective action introduces new errors.
Error correction rate	The error correction rate can be used with the error detection rate to indicate how many known errors are to be corrected. It is also used to aid in resource management.

Table 7.1   (Continued)

Metric	Description
Severe error detection rate	The severe error detection rate is used to estimate reliability based only on the occurrence of severe errors.
Severe error correction rate	This metric is used to measure the responsiveness of the correction process to severe errors. This metric as well as the three metrics described above are useful to both management and software engineers and can be used on all projects.
Errors per location	Errors tracked according to function or subfunction to determine if one area of the code is more error-prone.
Criticality of errors	Classifying the severity of errors will shed light on whether the errors have the potential for mission or safety loss and will also aid in scheduling of corrective action.
Number and percentage of severe errors	This metric will indicate how many of the errors must be corrected immediately and also can be used to perform projections of only severe errors as opposed to those that are severe and negligible.
Structural complexity per location	This metric may be used in with other metrics to determine what, if any, impact a certain level of complexity has on errors generated.

Table 7.1   (Continued)

Metric	Description
Functional complexity per location	This metric may be used in with other metrics to determine what, if any, impact a certain level of complexity has on errors generated.

Table 7.2   Summary of Software Product Metrics

Metric	Description
Number and percentage of modules that perform more than or only one function	This metric will indicate the cohesiveness of the overall design.
Number and percentage of modules that have a high structural complexity	This metric will indicate if the overall design may need to be redesigned to reduce complexity. This should be used with the previous metric to determine if the high complexity is due to complex functionality, which indicates a lack of cohesiveness, or if the high complexity is due to many case statements and/or error trapping, which is for the most part unavoidable.
Number and percentage of modules that have exactly one entrance and one exit	This metric is a very good indicator of a cohesive design. It should be used if structured

Table 7.2   (Continued)

Metric	Description
	design practices are not completely in use.
Number and percentage of modules that are documented according to standards	This metric may be used when a maintainability problem is suspected.
Number and percentage of modules that are traceable to written requirements	This metric is an important one because it allows the developers to determine if the code contains all of the requirements and addresses the requirements completely.
Number and percentage of errors that are found in reused code	This metric should be used if reused code is used and it is suspected that the code may not be performing reliably.

Table 7.3   Summary of Software Process Metrics

Metric	Description
Errors introduced by phase	As each error is detected, it can be determined at which phase of the life cycle it was probably introduced. This is to determine which phase, if any, is more responsible for errors.
Errors detected by phase	By tracking at which phase the error was found, and also tracking the previous metric, it can be determined that the delay is for finding bugs once introduced. This metric also shows if errors are being found before they become costly.
Total time spent in analysis	This metric should be used with the same metric for the other

Table 7.3 (Continued)

Metric	Description
	phases of the life cycle to determine which phase(s) are using the most resources. If a structured approach is taken, the time spent in analysis should be greater than in many of the other phases of the life cycle.
Total time spent in design	This metric should be used with the same metric for the other phases of the life cycle to determine which phase(s) are using the most resources. If a structured approach is taken, the time spent designing will be greater than the time spent in many of the other phases of the life cycle.
Total time spent in coding	This metric should be used with the same metric for the other phases of the life cycle to determine which phase(s) are using the most resources. If a structured approach is taken this time will be much less than the analysis and design times.
Total time spent in unit testing	This metric should be used with the same metric for the other phases of the life cycle to determine which phase(s) are using the most resources. The time spent in unit testing will probably be greater than the time spent in system testing if a structured approach is used. This is because lower level errors are to be found in this

Table 7.3 (Continued)

Metric	Description
	phases before system test begins.
Total time spent in systems testing	This metric should be used with the same metric for the other phases of the life cycle determine which phase(s) are using the most resources. Ideally, if a structured approach has been used throughout the life cycle, the time spent in system testing will be not as high as the time spent in analysis, design or unit testing. This time, however, depends on the nature of the product. Some products may not be adequately tested in laboratory.
Total maintenance time	This time is computed by summing the times of all maintenance actions (including fault isolation and administrative time). It is used to compare with the other life-cycle phase times and is also used for the other metrics below.
Average maintenance administration time	This metric indicates how much time is spent performing administrative duties before and after the error is even corrected. This includes the time spent assigning the error to the appropriate person, verifying the error, and releasing the correction in a new version.
Average corrective action time	The average time spent on a corrective action should be

Table 7.3 (Continued)

Metric	Description
	tracked and should include time spent isolating the fault.
Reason for corrective action	This is an extremely important metric for determining the source of errors. Some reasons are (1) previous maintenance action, (2) new requirement, (3) requirement change, (4) misinterpreted requirement, (5) missing requirement, (6) ambiguous requirement, (7) change in software environment, (8) change in hardware environment, (9) code/logic error, (10) performance error, (11) other. This metric should be in the form of a distribution of each of the above types.
Maximum, minimum, and median corrective action times	The maximum, minimum, and median corrective action times should be tracked so in addition to the distribution of maintenance actions per some defined interval. For example, knowing 20% of the maintenance actions took > 1 day, 40% took > 0.75 days and 40% took >0.5 days, the maximum was 3 days and the minimum was 0.1 days, is more valuable than knowing that the average is 0.72 days.
Cost of corrective action	This cost can be determined by the multiplying the average corrective action time (including fault isolation and the average administration time

Table 7.3   (Continued)

Metric	Description
	spent) by the development cost per hour (may be charging cost).
Milestone, start, and release dates	This metric is necessary for all projects to determine whether or not major milestones are being met. The start and release dates must be known to be used by many of the other metrics and models.
Historical data	All of the data described in this chapter and all results of using any metrics described and any models described in the next chapter should be kept as historical data from one project to the next. This is one of the most critical pieces of data to collect.
Time spent in inspection and walkthrough	The total time spent doing design and code inspections and walkthroughs should be tracked, particularly if it is suspected that many errors are being introduced in early phases but not detected until later phases.
Number of action items implemented from inspection and walkthrough	This metric should be used if the previous metric is used to ensure that time is not being wasted in walkthroughs and inspections and that action items are taken and responded to.
Percentage of functions tested and verified	This is a test coverage metric and should be used in conjunction with the next two test coverage

Table 7.3 (Continued)

Metric	Description
	metrics to determine if testing is efficient. This particular test coverage metric will determine if sufficient requirements and functional testing is being performed.
Percentage of independent paths tested and verified	This test coverage metric will determine if sufficient structural testing is being completed.
Percentage of source lines of code tested and verified	This test coverage metric will determine if all of the code is being covered in testing.

REFERENCES

Dunn, Robert, and Ulman, Richard. *Quality Assurance for Computer Software*, McGraw-Hill, New York, 1982.

Grady, R., and Caswell, D. *Software Metrics: Establishing a Company Wide Program*, Hewlett-Packard Company, Prentice-Hall, Englewood Cliffs, NJ, 1987.

IEEE Standard Dictionary of Measures to Produce Reliable Software, IEEE Standard 981, IEEE Publications, New York, 1988.

IEEE Guide for the Use of IEEE Standard Dictionary of Measures to Produce Reliable Software, IEEE Standard 982, IEEE Publications, New York, 1988.

CHAPTER 8

Software Reliability Models

The objectives of a software reliability model are to evaluate software quantitatively; provide development status, test status, and schedule status; and monitor reliability performance and changes in reliability performance of the software.

There have been many reliability models developed in the last two decades. Many of these models have been invalidated because of invalid assumptions, inaccuracy, or impracticality or costliness. This chapter provides an overview of a cross section of various types of models used for predicting software reliability.

Many of the models developed to date are based on error counts and do not directly model the software development environment. These models often assume an exponential error rate. There are a few models that attempt to model software reliability based on certain design factors that exist during the software development process. Software reliability models may model fault introduction, fault removal, and the environment. Some models attempt to simulate error introduction with error tagging techniques.

Many of the models are estimators because they are used primarily during the test phase and are continually updated as data are collected. A few models are predictive, actually predicting the reliability before the coding even begins.

A good model must have assumptions valid for the particular development process for which it will be used. Before a model is implemented, the assumptions must be verified as consistent with what is expected to be experienced on the project. If it is not known which of the models most closely fits the current project, it may be wise to implement more than one model and analyze the results or to implement models based on historical data from a similar product. It is a good idea to implement more than one model on a given project even if information is available on the product.

A good model will not only have assumptions that are valid for the project it is implemented on, it will be practical. If a model is not practical, it may have an undesirable effect on the development process. The accuracy of the results may be outweighed by the cost of using the model.

A good model is also relatively easy to implement. This is a subset of being practical. A good model should not need an extensive amount of resources such as computing power and specialized personnel to implement. A good model should have inputs that can be collected without an extensive amount of manpower or resources.

For each of the models we discuss how the model is implemented, at what point in the life cycle it is implemented, how practical the model is, and the expected results of the model and how they may be applied to the real world.

8.1 SOFTWARE RELIABILITY MODEL PARAMETERS

There are many software reliability models existing today that were developed by various authors. These models use various parameters that the author has redefined so that the models may be discussed in this chapter with consistent use of variable names. The variable names are as follows:

ETF: Total number of inherent errors in the software. This number is assumed to be fixed and finite.

ETV: Total number of inherent errors in the software. The number is assumed to be variable because of the possibility of inserting new errors into the code over time.

EC(t): Total number of errors corrected at some point in time, or after some usage or testing time t has elapsed.

ED(t): Total number of errors detected at some point in time, or after some usage or testing time t has elapsed.

p: Number of testing periods or intervals. This is the number of intervals between an error correction activity. Some models assume that errors are corrected as soon as they are detected, or that p = ED(t) = EC(t).

EC(p): Number of errors corrected up through the pth testing period. This would not include the errors corrected during the pth test period. This may be different from EC(t) if more than one error is corrected during any p interval.

θ: Acceleration of errors, or the change in the failure intensity.

t: Testing or usage time accumulated up to present time or present number of detected errors.

τ: Execution time accumulated.

k: Constant of proportionality.

λ_0: Initial failure rate.

λ_p: Present failure rate.

α: Growth rate.

$I(t)$: Estimated number of lines of executable code at testing or usage time t.

N: Total number of test cases run.

S: Total number of successful test cases run.

8.2 THE MUSA MODELS

Dr. John Musa of Bell Laboratories has been developing software reliability models for the last two decades. He has joined his research with that of Kazuhira Okumoto and Anthony Iannino, who are also of Bell Laboratories, and has developed two models called the logarithmic model and the basic model.

8.2.1 The Basic Model

The basic model assumes that errors contribute equally to the error rate and that the error rate declines uniformly for every error corrected. This means that the error rate over time is constant. It is assumed that there is a finite number of estimated total inherent errors in the software. This number is not necessarily fixed, however, meaning that the model can account for errors generated during error correction. The following parameters define the Musa basic model:

$$\lambda_p = \lambda_0 \exp \frac{(-\lambda_0\tau)}{ETV)}$$

Section 8.3 shows how ETV is estimated. For scheduling purposes, it is possible to project the number of errors that must be found to reach some reliability objective and also the execution time needed to reach that objective. The author has found these projections to be useful in projecting manpower requirements as well as the ability to reach a release date with the required estimated number of inherent errors. These equations are as follows:

Number of errors to be found to reach some error rate objective

$$= \frac{\lambda_0}{\lambda_0 \ln(\lambda_p/\lambda_f)}$$

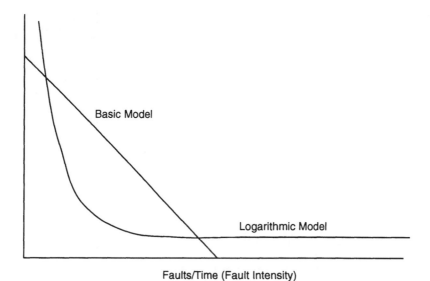

Figure 8.1   Fault intensity assumptions for Musa models.

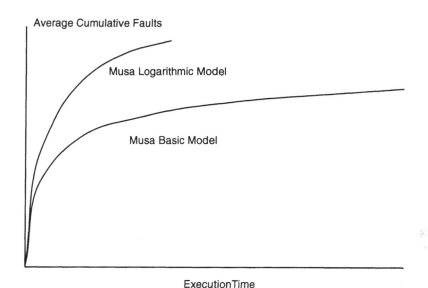

Figure 8.2 Cumulative fault assumptions for Musa models.

Execution time needed to reach an error rate objective
$$- \lambda_0 / \lambda_0 (\lambda_p - \lambda_f)$$

See Figures 8.1, 8.2, and 8.3 for an illustration of the assumptions of the Musa models.

8.2.2   The Logarithmic Model

The logarithmic model differs from the basic model in that it assumes that errors contribute differently to error rate. It assumes that errors that exist in frequently executed code will be found earlier, causing larger decreases in the error rate over time. Therefore, the error rate over time is not constant, as it is with the basic model. It also assumes that the total inherent number of errors is infinite. The following are the parameters for the logarithmic model:

$$\lambda_p = \frac{\lambda_0}{\lambda_0 \theta \tau + 1}$$

In order to project the number of errors needed to be found to reach an error rate objective or to project the execution time needed to reach an error rate objective, use the following equations:

Cumulative Errors Detected

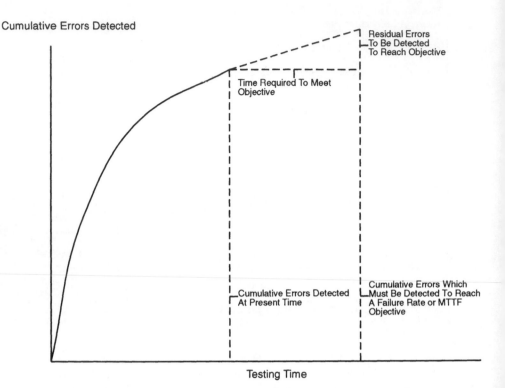

Figure 8.3 Projecting testing time or number of detected errors to reach an objective.

Number of errors to be found to reach the error rate objective

$$= \frac{1}{\ln\left(\frac{\lambda_p}{\lambda_f}\right)}$$

Execution time needed to reach an error rate objective

$$= \frac{1}{1/\lambda_f - 1/\lambda_p}$$

8.3   SHOOMAN'S MODEL

Martin Shooman of the New York Polytechnical Institute has done extensive research in the software reliability field. The Shooman model is a binomial model. This model assumes that there is a finite and fixed number of estimated total inherent errors in the software. The error rate is assumed to be constant over time. This model does not consider the effects of introducing errors due to maintenance or the possibility that errors that exist in frequently executed portions of the software may be found earlier than others. Instead, it assumes that over time the effect of these types of errors will average out. It also assumes that the errors will be removed immediately.

The Shooman model should be used after the start of systems integration testing. It has been shown to be more effective if used later in the life cycle. The main reason for this is that earlier in development, particularly during debugging and unit test, the error rate will probably be increasing over time (as with hardware burn-in). The Shooman model cannot be used if this is the case. The following are the parameters of the Shooman model:

$$MTTF(t) = \frac{1}{k[ETF/I(t) - EC(t)/I(t)]}$$

$$R(t) = \exp(-\{k [ETF - EC(t)]t\})$$

As can be seen from these parameters, the Shooman model accounts for the possibility that the volume of the software as shown by the lines of code estimated may fluctuate over the course of the project. The line-of-code parameter is intended to normalize this effect. The author used this model on software that had negligible fluctuation in volume and assumed the line-of-code estimate to be 1.

At this point you are probably wondering how ETF and ETV are estimated. The procedure for making this estimate requires that the fault intensity be plotted versus the total number of cumulative errors. In order for ETF or ETV to be finite, this plot must form a progression from the lower right to the top left. To determine ETV and ETF the best straight line must be drawn through the points to reach a Y intercept. This Y intercept is the total estimated number of errors. It is either variable or fixed, depending on the model chosen. Figure 8.4 illustrates this. The value of K can be derived by calculating the negative inverse of the slope of that line. Either the least-squares estimate or the maximum-likelihood estimate may be used to draw the best straight line through these points.

There are other techniques for estimating these two unknowns, such as simultaneous equations; however, the author has found this technique to be the most practical. The graph should be drawn at more than

Cumulative Number of Faults

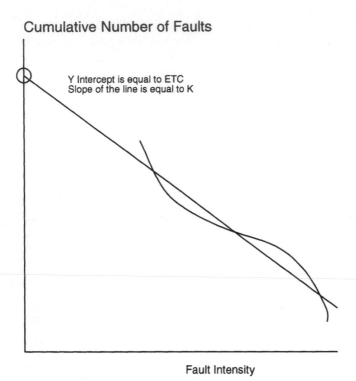

Figure 8.4   Predicting K and ETC.

one point during the testing process, since the accuracy improves with more data points accumulated

8.4   JELINSKI–MORANDA DEUTROPHICATION MODEL

Paul L. Jelinski and Z. Moranda have spent many years researching software reliability and developing models, the deutrophication model being one of the best known. If the following assumptions are maintained:

1. Errors are corrected as soon as detected.
2. Only one error is corrected at a time.
3. There is a constant number of lines of code.

then this model is identical to the Shooman model. In this case, $p = ED(t) = EC(t)$. The parameters for the Jelinski–Moranda model are:

$$MTTF(t) = \frac{1}{k[ETF - ED(t)]}$$

$$R(t) = \exp(-\{k[ETF - ED(t)]t\})$$

If, on the other hand, the errors are not assumed to be corrected as soon as detected, this model will yield results different from those of the Shooman model. However, a true binomial model should make the assumption that errors are removed as soon as they are detected.

8.5 LIPOW MODIFIED JELINSKI–MORANDA MODEL

M. Lipow has been developing various software reliability models, particularly in the acrospace industry. The Lipow model makes one modification to the Jelinski–Moranda model. It assumes that errors may not be corrected immediately when discovered. This modification was made to more closely model what usually happens during a real-life development project. When software reliability models were first developed, they were validated with laboratory experiments. The software used in many of the experiments was developed more or less in a vacuum without the presence of real-life factors. The fact that errors are not removed as soon as they are detected was one factor that was not modeled in the earlier experiments. The parameters for the Lloyd–Lipow model are as follows:

$$MTTF(t) = \frac{1}{k[ETF - EC(p)]}$$

$$R(t) = \exp(-\{k[ETF - EC(p)]\})$$

In a survey conducted by Donald Reifer and Associates, it was found that out of 98 companies, 50% of all those companies that employed reliability modeling had implemented the Lipow model, and most of these were in the aerospace industry.

8.6 GOEL–OKUMOTO MODEL

Amrit Goel of Syracuse University and Kazuhira Okumoto of Bell Laboratories both have years of experience in developing software reliability models. The Goel–Okumoto model assumes that the distribution of errors is not homogeneous over time. This model is best used during the earlier phases of the life cycle, since nonhomogeneous distribution of errors is most likely to occur earlier as opposed to during the operational phase. This model assumes that errors may not be removed as soon as they are discovered and that errors may cause other errors. The parameters of the Goel–Okumoto model are:

$$\lambda(t) = ab \exp(-bt)$$

where a and b are determined by solving the following equations:

$$\frac{ED(t)}{a} = 1 - \exp(-bt)$$

$$\frac{ED(t)}{b} = at \exp(-bt) + \sum_{i=1}^{n} t_i$$

Note that a is a constant and b is in terms of errors per time. To make an initial estimate of a and b, the author has either used various software tools to solve both equations or made an initial estimate of a and b to be k and ETF, respectively, and iteratively solved the equations.

8.7   JELINSKI–MORANDA GEOMETRIC DEUTROPHICATION MODEL

The Jelinski–Moranda geometric deutrophication model is intended to be used when error data are available only in periodic form. It assumes that the failure rate between error occurrences forms a geometric progression and that the failure rate remains constant during any one interval.

This model is useful when the amount of error data cannot be collected very often or when the resources to do so do not exist. The following are the parameters of the geometric model: D is the initial error rate during period 1, kD is the error rate when first error is found, k is always positive and less than 1, and

$$R(t) = \exp(-DK^p t)$$

Before the first error has been detected, D cannot be estimated and is assumed to be infinite. In the other intervals D and k are estimated as:

$$D = ED(t) / \sum_{i=1}^{ED(t)} k^{i-1} t_i$$

$$\frac{\sum\limits_{i=1}^{\text{ED}(t)} ik^i t_i}{\sum\limits_{i=1}^{\text{ED}(t)} k^i t_i} = \frac{\text{ED}(t) + 1}{2}$$

8.8 DUANE GROWTH MODEL

The Duane growth model has been used on hardware for many years and has been applied to software in an effort to determine the rate at which the error rate improves over time. The parameters of the Duane growth model are:

$$\lambda_\Sigma = Kt^{-\alpha}$$

If the Duane growth model is used on many projects, then an organization may be able to develop an objective or standard growth rate to compare against. A growth rate is also helpful in projecting reliability of the product at some future time.

8.9 SCHICK–WOLVERTON MODEL

George Schick and Ray Wolverton have developed a model that assumes a Raleigh distribution for the time between error occurrences, as opposed to an exponential distribution. The Raleigh distribution assumes that the error rate is proportional to the number of errors remaining and the time spent testing or debugging. The Schick–Wolverton model assumes that errors are immediately removed when discovered.

The Raleigh distribution is a form of the Weibull distribution and in practical terms assumes that the error rate changes based on three variables or unknowns. The Raleigh distribution assumes that one of these variables is set to 2, therefore leaving two unknowns to solve for. The parameters of the Schick–Wolverton model are:

$$\text{MTTF}(t) = \sqrt{\frac{\pi}{2k(\text{ETF} - p)}}$$

$$R(t) = \exp\left[\frac{-k(\text{ETF} - p)t^2}{2}\right]$$

The two unknowns of the Schick–Wolverton model are solved for as follows:

$$k = \frac{2\text{ED}(t)}{\sum\limits_{i=1}^{\text{ED}(t)} [\text{ETF} - (i - 1)]t^2}$$

$$\sum_{i=1}^{\text{ED}(t)} \frac{1}{[\text{ETF} - (i - 1)]} = \frac{k \sum\limits_{i=1}^{\text{ED}(t)} t^2}{2}$$

This model assumes that $p = \text{ED}(t) = \text{EC}(t)$; therefore, there is only one error occurrence per interval and t is the cumulative time to detect $\text{ED}(t) = p = \text{EC}(t)$, the number of errors.

8.10   LEONE TEST COVERAGE MODEL

The author presents a new method of estimating the reliability of software based on the completion and coverage of certain development and test tasks. This software reliability model, the Leone test coverage model, is relatively simple to implement, lending itself to be a useful management, development, or testing tool, as well as a reliability measure.

All the inputs for this model are collected during testing and thus should be readily accessible if effective software engineering practices are in place. If they are not, this model will aid in pointing out the required areas of improvement with respect to software development and engineering. This measurement model is microscopic; it takes into account the actual structure of the software, as opposed to macroscopic models, which consider only the errors that are detected. The four essential inputs to the model are as follows:

1. The percentage of total executable lines of code that are tested and validated.
2. The percentage of independent test paths that are tested and validated (note that this does *not* mean all possible test paths; independent test path will be further defined later).
3. The percentage of functions/requirements that are tested and validated.
4. The percentage of hazard test cases that are tested and validated. These are test cases proving that the software does not perform an undesirable function. Undesirable and unexpected functions arc data corruption, failure of the software to detect erroneous conditions, software detecting erroneous conditions that are not erro-

neous, and others; see Chapter 11 for information on constructing these types of test cases.

8.10.1   Assumptions of the Model

The assumptions of the Leone test coverage model are as follows:

1. Software reliability has a direct relationship with testing completion and coverage. This essentially means that if some particular function or area of the software has not been validated, then it is not assumed to be functional.
2. The model quantifies software characteristics that may appear to be intangible.
3. According to the model, software that has 100% of every executable line of code validated, 100% of each independent path validated, and 100% of each function validated (assuming repair) will perform successfully.
4. The model is used from the start of unit testing to the end of acceptance testing.

The objectives for using this model are as follows:

1. To identify a relative measure of the work that must be completed to reach a specific reliability objective.
2. To identify problem areas in testing that might need special attention (such as manpower or test case development adjustments).
3. To provide feedback directly to the development and test effort.
4. To aid in effective and efficient validation of software.
5. To provide management with a software engineering tool that is practical, to perform the first four objectives.

8.10.2   Parameters of the Model

The four essential inputs for this model are lines of executable code validated, independent test paths validated, functions/requirements, and hazard test cases validated. Four weighting parameters are also used. Each of the four inputs can be determined from various sources, including automated tools and software reviews.

The probability of the software performing successfully according to the software requirements at some point in time is shown as:

F1 = W1 × (percent of total executable lines of code that have
         been tested during any integration/systems/acceptance test
         and validated)

F2 = W2 × (percent of total independent test paths that have been
         tested during any unit/integration/systems/acceptance test and
         validated)

F3 = W3 × (percent of total functions/requirements that have been
         tested during any unit/integration/systems/acceptance test and
         validated)

F4 = W4 × (percent of total hazard test paths that have been
         tested during any unit/integration/systems/acceptance test and
         validated)

$$R = (F1 + F2 + F3 + F4)/ 4$$
$$W1 + W2 + W3 + W4 = 4$$

Note the definition "any unit/integration/systems/acceptance test."
This implies that some executable line of code can be tested in the same
test case as some independent path and as some function/requirement.
The ideal situation would be to have the minimum number of test cases
covering the most amount of source lines of code, test paths, and functions.

Inspection of the model shows that inefficient test coverage will probably not produce desirable results. It is important to remember that only
those tests that are validated as performing correctly are counted. Any
test case that did not perform correctly would have to be corrected and
revalidated to be counted in the model.

The best way to estimate the percentage of lines of code tested is to
obtain or develop an automated tool that will count all of the total lines
of code in the source models. This is fairly easy to develop and should be
used anyway for software management. During development of test
cases the lines of code executed by that test case could be used for software management. During development of test cases the lines of code
executed by that test case can be defined. Some test tools will even count
the lines of code that have been tested.

To determine the independent test paths, you will need to refer to
structured design and test methodologies such as McCabe's for detailed
information (see Chapter 9).

Briefly summarized, the number of independent test paths is equal to the number of decision points in the logic of the code plus one. The decision points in logic are the if, case, repeat, while, loop, and other statements that cause the logic of the software to branch in one or more directions. A test case must be developed for each branch in logic. Remember that the number of independent test cases is not equal to the number of all possible paths. The distinction must be clear, since for a medium- or large-sized software program the total number of all possible paths would be, for all practical purposes, unmeasurable in terms of testing. These independent test cases would already be developed if structured design, code, test, and maintenance are employed.

Measuring the number of functions tested may not be as straightforward as measuring the other two parameters necessary for the model. The author suggests a test case for every written requirement and for every functional test case described in Chapter 10.

The hazards test cases are determined from a fault tree analysis or a failure modes effect and criticality analysis (FMECA).

The weight parameters are used when the contribution of each parameter to the reliability of the software is known to be not equal. If you do not know the relative relationships between each of the three parameters and their effect on software reliability, then assume each weight equals 1. On the other hand, if you know from past experience or historical data that one or more of these factors contributes to the reliability of the software more than the others, then set the weights accordingly.

Software that is being developed for the first time or is new technology will probably have the function/requirements parameter weighted more heavily than the others. Software that is intensely user interactive may also have that weight be heavier. However, software that is clearly defined but structurally (not functionally) complex would probably have the test path parameter weighted to be heavier. Software that is safety or mission critical may have the fourth parameter weighted more heavily. For any kind of application testing, every line of source code will probably be important with respect to these three parameters.

The Leone test coverage model is relatively simple to implement and can and should be implemented with other design and test methodologies and tools, as well as being used as a reliability measurement. The data used as inputs to the model are data that would be readily accessible, particularly if the software is being designed and tested according to structured methods.

If structured methods are not employed, this model will help to isolate areas for improvement. This model differs from some of the other
existing software reliability models in that it attempts to isolate how
software is or becomes reliable, as opposed to estimating the software's
reliability based on error counts that do not take into account how or
why the error occurred.

8.11 ERROR SEEDING MODELS

Seeding is the act of inserting errors into software in order to estimate
the total number of inherent errors in the software. The author strongly
recommends that seeding not be implemented. However, seeding is discussed because there are other models that were adapted from the seeding concept.

Oddly enough, the error seeding concept originated with fish tagging.
In order to determine how many fish were in a body of water, some fish
were tagged. The ratio of the fish caught that were tagged to the total
number of tagged fish was assumed to be the same as the relationship
between the total fish caught and the total number of fish in the pond.

Error seeding models require that errors be inserted into the software
during the testing phase. The errors seeding must be representative of
real errors that would be found during normal testing. Seeded errors
must be randomly chosen and must cover the source code uniformly.
This is a contradiction of terms since *random* implies that the portion of
the source code where the error is inserted is unknown. Blocking would
be used to assure that errors are random and do cover a cross section of
the source code. Blocking means dividing the source code into sections
and then randomly inserting errors into each section.

The parameters of the seeding model are as follows:

V = total number of seeded errors

v = number of seeded errors that were detected by the testers

$ED(t)$ = nonseeded errors detected by the testers

ETV = total number of inherent nonseeded errors

$$\frac{ED(t)}{ETV} = \frac{v}{V}$$

The relationship between seeded errors found and seeded errors
known to exist in the software is assumed to be equal to the relationship

of the number of nonseeded errors found to the total number of errors that exist. The parameter N is the only unknown in this model. If the testers have found only a small portion of the total seeded errors that were inserted, then the model assumes that only a small portion of all of the inherent errors has been found.

Seeded errors must not be obvious to the testers or the users or the seeding model is useless. The seeded errors must also be documented and removed as soon as possible so that no new errors are generated by these seeded errors. This presents a bigger problem than may be imagined.

Suppose that errors are randomly and discretely inserted into the software and the testers test using this version of software. Now let us say that at the end of testing we must assure that all the seeded errors are removed. It may seem that the obvious solution is to simply edit the source code and remove the errors. However, it is probable that during this time changes have been made to other parts of the code that may have an effect on the code in which the error was inserted. It is also possible that these seeded errors prevented some real errors from being detected. Therefore, we would be forced to decide between recalling the software in its original form prior to the error insertion and making all the error corrections that were made during testing to this version, or attempting to remove the errors from the tested version and taking a chance on missing some or adversely affecting code that was already tested. In either case we would be doing more work than necessary or desirable and would be taking a big risk of actually adversely affecting the reliability of the software when removing the errors from it.

Management as well as the customer may not like the idea of errors being inserted into software. The testers themselves may not be overjoyed if they realize they are testing software with unnatural errors in it.

For all of these reasons, seeding is not suggested by this author as a means of estimating software reliability. However, there is a model based on the seeding concept that can be suggested as a possible one to be implemented.

8.12 DUAL TEST GROUP MODEL

The dual test group model was used for many years as a statistical tool before being applied to software. The dual test group model assumes that the actual seeding process just defined is replaced with two independent simultaneous test groups. Instead of relating the seeded errors found to the nonseeded errors found, we will compare the errors found by one test group with errors found by another equally competent test group.

The first assumption of this model is that the two test groups are about equal in experience and number. It also assumes that each test group is testing the same version of software. The test groups must be independent in that they are not aware of what errors are detected by the other test group or even of errors or rate of errors found by the other test group.

If these assumptions hold true, then one of the following is assumed to occur:

1. Both groups will uncover the same errors if there are not many residual errors left in the software.
2. Both groups will uncover different errors if there are many residual errors in the software.

We must track the number of errors that are commonly found by both test group 1 and test group 2; see Figure 8.5 for a graphical representation of the model.

The parameters of the dual test group are defined as:

$$\text{ETV} = \frac{ED_{12}}{E_1 + E_2}$$

where

ED_1 = the number of errors discovered solely by test group 1
ED_2 = the number of errors discovered solely by test group 2
ED_{12} = the number of errors found by both test group 1 and 2
$E_1 = ED_{12}/ED_2$
$ED_2 = ED_{12}/ED_1$

One drawback to this model is the case when each test group inputs completely different test cases testing different portions of the code. Imagine test group 1 testing half of the subprograms and test group 2 testing the other half. There would probably not be many common errors found, particularly if the design were structured to be modular, as it should be. In this case the model would be pessimistic since both test groups combined may have found many errors but the number found commonly is small (see Fig. 8.6).

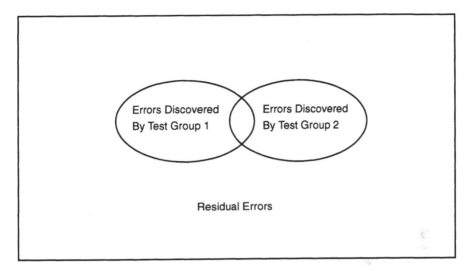

Figure 8.5   Dual test group model—basic assumptions of the model.

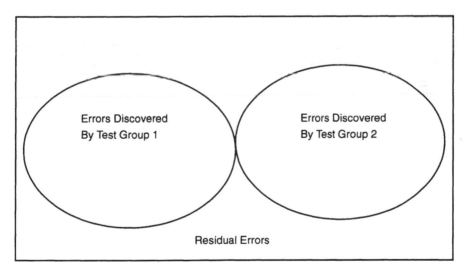

Figure 8.6   Dual test group model—case of efficient testers and test cases with no coverage overlap.

Another drawback to this model is that if both test groups input identical test cases, then the model may not be accurate since some tests may be completely overlooked by both groups. The model will probably be optimistic in this case (see Fig. 8.7).

If the assumption of equal experience among test groups is not valid, then it is possible the model will be pessimistic. If test group 1 is much more capable of finding errors than test group 2, then the number of commonly found errors may not be very high, causing the prediction of the total number of inherent errors to be high (see Fig. 8.8).

8.13   TESTING SUCCESS MODEL

The testing success model is by far the simplest model presented in this book. The model is described as follows:

$$R = \frac{S}{N}$$

where S is the total number of successfully executed test cases and N is the total number of test cases executed.

This model makes the basic assumption that the probability of the software performing successfully is equal to the probability of implementing a successful test case. For this model to be relatively accurate requires that a success or fail status be collected for every test case executed. If the software is fixed, retested, and test cases that previously were not successful are not successful, then S would need to be updated while N remained constant, unless new test cases were introduced.

The test cases themselves would need to reflect the profile of the end user and would have to completely cover the source code. It is possible to employ blocking techniques that will ensure that the source code is covered to some extent. Blocking means that the source code is divided into portions, such as the primary functions, and that test cases are drawn randomly from each of the portions. Therefore, the test cases are randomly chosen but also cover all of the software functions.

This model may give an estimate of how reliable the software is at the current time; however, it will not project the reliability of the software at some future time.

8.14   WEIBULL MODEL

Another reliability model is the Weibull model. This model assumes a Weibull distribution of software faults. One advantage of using this

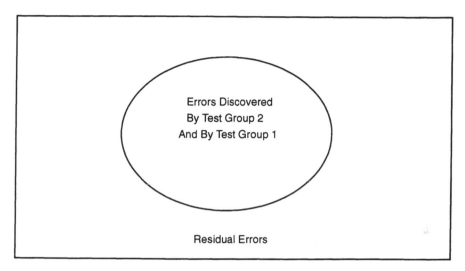

Figure 8.7 Dual test group model—case of inefficient testers or incomplete test coverage.

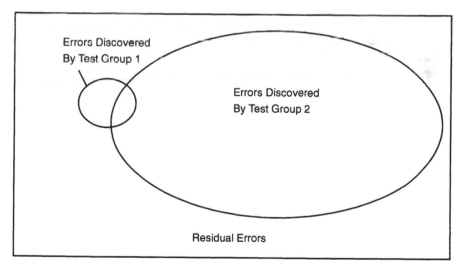

Figure 8.8 Dual test group model—case of test groups not equal in number or experience.

model is that the change in fault density may be positive, negative, or constant. Its parameters are:

$$\text{MTTF} = \frac{b}{a} \Gamma \frac{1}{a}$$

$$R(t) = \exp\left[-\frac{t^a}{b}\right]$$

where $a > 1$, or $a < 1$, or $a = 1$ and b is a constant of proportionality. The terms a and b must be determined using graphical procedures similar to the procedure used to estimate k and ETF or ETV. The author is currently investigating this model's application to real software development environments.

8.15   PREDICTIVE MODELS

The models shown so far are estimative models, as opposed to predictive. The predictive models use empirical as opposed to project data to predict, before coding even begins, what the reliability will be. The Mil-Hdbk 217-F uses empirical data to predict the reliability of electronic components based on some characteristics of the component. RADC has determined some relationships between software characteristics and reliability in the technical report TR-87-171.

In this report the three areas that determine software reliability are the application type, development environment, and characteristics of the software.

$$R = A \times D \times S$$

where

$$S = \text{SA} \times \text{ST} \times \text{SQ} \times \text{SL} \times \text{SM} \times \text{SX} \times \text{SR}$$

and where R is in terms of faults per executable lines of code, A is determined by using a look-up chart, and D is determined by answering questions in a checklist to determine how structured the development organization is. The term SA is an indication of how software anomalies are managed; ST is the requirements traceability indicator; and SQ is the quality indicator. Checklists are used to determine these values. Further, SL is the language indicator, SM is the modularity indicator, SX is the size indicator, and SR is the review indicator. These values are determined by look-up charts and checklists.

As discussed in previous chapters, the author has not found that errors per lines of code is a valid software reliability metric. Unfortunately, however, this prediction document is currently one of only a few prediction techniques generally available.

An organization may be able to determine its own empirical values, and therefore its own predictive measurement, by collecting data on its own programs and determining what relationship, if any, certain characteristics have with reliability. RADC collected data on the nine characteristics shown of this model. However, there may be and probably are more characteristics that may be quantified. The advantage to using the RADC guidelines is that RADC has collected data on a large cross section of projects. The disadvantage is that those projects may not represent your software project.

There is some skepticism in industry that it may not be possible to predict software reliability before it is developed. At this point in time that argument may be valid. However, as more data are collected on many types of software, and more research is conducted not only on software reliability but on software engineering, it may become possible to predict reliability for software with some confidence. The prediction techniques for electronic parts evolved and are still evolving in this manner.

8.16 CASE STUDIES OF RELIABILITY MODELS

The following are real case studies for each of the software programs that implemented software reliability models. These projects were described previously in Sections 7.4.1 through 7.4.4 in Chapter 7.

8.16.1 Reliability Modeling Case Study 1

This financial software of approximately 200,000 lines of PASCAL source code was developed and tested on two 8-hour shifts. The two shifts allowed for completely independent testing by completely independent groups. The error-tracking process was already tracking duplicate errors during the testing process, so that all that was required to use the dual test group model was an impartial person (not on either test group) to analyze the reports that were duplicates and then determine how many were cross-test-group duplicates.

The dual test group model was used during the 12-week testing period, and the results are shown in Figure 8.9. The total number of inherent errors estimated to exist in the software was calculated to be

$$\text{ETV} = \frac{1077(372)}{93} = 4308 \text{ inherent errors}$$

This is a very high estimate, considering that the software was small-to medium-sized in volume. By the twelfth week of testing, 1356 unique errors had been discovered and the rate of detection was not leveling off.

The least-squares estimate was used to determine the total number of inherent errors by plotting the fault intensity versus the cumulative faults. The graph is shown in Figure 8.10, and the results were used to solve for the Shooman and Musa basic models.

$$\text{ED}(t) = \text{EC}(t) = 1356$$

(It was not known when the errors were corrected, so correction was assumed to be immediate.)

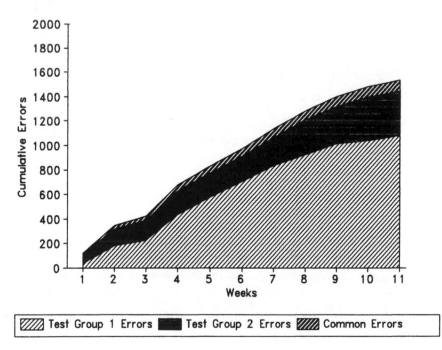

Figure 8.9   Test group 1, test group 2, common errors.

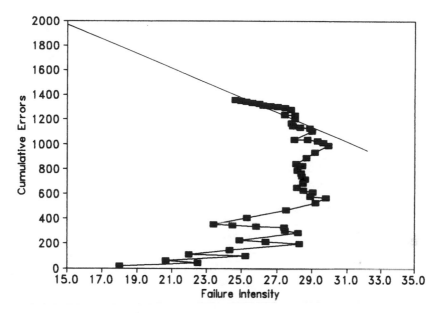

Figure 8.10 Cumulative errors versus failure intensity.

$$K = 0.017$$

$$\text{ETF} = \text{ETV} = 1979 \qquad \text{(from the plot)}$$

$$t = 54 \text{ days}$$

$$\text{MTTF}_{\text{Shooman}} = \frac{1}{0.017(1979 - 1356)} = 0.094420 \text{ days}$$

$$\lambda_{\text{Basic}} = 29 \exp\left[\frac{-29\,(54)}{1979}\right]$$

$$= 13.144285 \text{ failures/day}$$

The RADC prediction methodologies were used by filling out the checklists and collecting metrics on the software. The results were:

$$R = A \times D \times S = 0.0110$$

$$A = 0.0058$$

$$D = 0.8542$$

$$S = (0.9)\,(1.1)\,(1)\,(1)\,(1)\,(1.5)\,(1.5)$$

$$\text{ETV} = 0.0110 \times 200{,}000 = 2200 \text{ faults}$$

This result is slightly higher than the 1979 determined by the graphical plot but lower than the 4308 determined by the dual test group. The result of 2200 was mostly due to a low development score, which was determined by a ckecklist procedure. This checklist includes many of the activities that have been found to be necessary to develop reliable software.

The software was released at the last point in time shown in the illustrations. Eventually, more than 2000 errors were detected. At that point it was decided to scrap the software; therefore, the RADC estimate and the dual test group model estimate could not be validated for certain. It was known, however, that the rate of error detection never became stable or leveled off; therefore, it was assumed that the RADC prediction was optimistic.

8.16.2   Reliability Modeling Case Study 2

The cumulative number of errors detected over time and the total number of estimated inherent errors in this real time software program consisting of 300,000 lines of FORTRAN are shown in Figures 8.11 and 8.12. Figure 8.12 shows that the change in the fault density is positive. Because of this, the fault count models such as the Shooman and Musa models were not used. The RADC prediction methodology was used by collecting data and using the checklists. The results were:

$$R = A \times D \times S = 0.0385$$
$$A = 0.009$$
$$D = 3.0846$$
$$S = (1.1) \ (1) \ (1) \ (1.4) \ (0.9) \ (1) \ (1)$$
$$\text{ETV} = 0.0385 \times 300,000 = 11550 \text{ faults}$$

The reason for the high total estimated number of errors is that product scored fair on the development metric and fair on the software characteristic metrics. The reliability prediction would be improved by improving these metrics.

8.16.3   Reliability Modeling Case Study 3

The Shooman, Musa, and prediction models were used for this insurance software consisting of 100,000 lines of C code. Figure 8.13 and 8.14 show the cumulative number of errors detected over time and the total number of inherent errors estimated in the software.

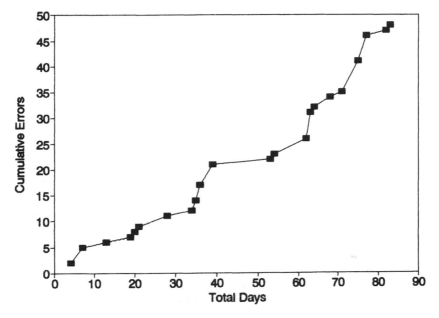

Figure 8.11 Total days versus cumulative errors.

The results of the models are:

$K = 0.0667$ (found by plot)
$ET = 29$ (found by plot)
$EC(t) = ED(t) = 23$

(It was not known when the errors were corrected so it was assumed to be immediate.)

$\lambda_0 = 1.0$ (first fault density)
$\theta = 0.9$ (change in fault density)

$$MTTF_{Shooman} = \frac{1}{0.0667(29 - 23)} = 2.498751 \text{ days}$$

$$\lambda_{Basic} = 1.0 \exp\left[\frac{-1.0(380)}{29}\right]$$
$$= 0.000002 \text{ failures/day}$$

$$\lambda_{Logarithmic} = \frac{1.0}{(1.0)(0.9)(380) + 1}$$
$$= 0.002916 \text{ failures / day}$$

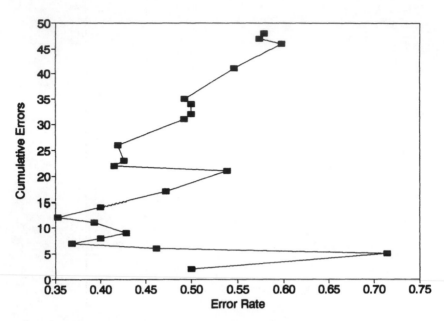

Figure 8.12   Error rate versus cumulative errors.

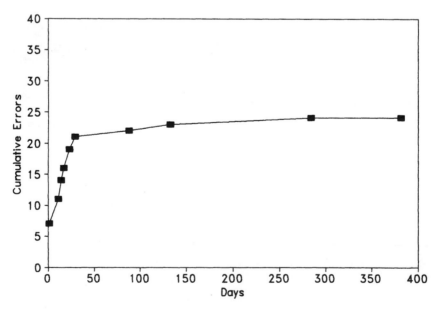

Figure 8.13   Cumulative errors versus days.

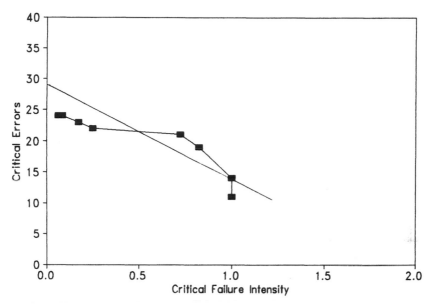

Figure 8.14 Critical errors versus failure intensity.

It was determined that because of the very small number of inherent errors predicted in the software, the Shooman model was likely to be pessimistic until the last error is detected. The results of the Musa logarithmic and Musa basic models were different by a factor of over 1000. It was determined that the logarithmic model best represented the development environment because the change in the fault density was not constant.

The results of the RADC prediction were:

$R = A \times D \times S = 0.0217$

$A = 0.0058$

$D = 0.8381$

$S = (0.9) (1.1) (1) (1) (2) (1.5) (1.5)$

ETV = $0.0217 \times 100{,}000 = 2170$ faults

This test case is one of the more interesting ones in that the software was shown to exhibit only 27 errors over a testing time of more than 1 year. However, the RADC prediction estimates 2170! This is an example of how software could be developed without adhering to the methodologies described in TR-87-171 and still be reliable.

The results of this prediction were low due to the D factor. This was because there were very few formal procedures used during the development of this software. The development group consisted of only two people for this project. Therefore the lack of these methods had little impact on the end reliability of the software. The RADC methods were clearly intended for larger software programs.

8.16.4   Reliability Modeling Case Study 4

This engineering tool consisted of 400,000 lines of C code and was released in four distinct versions with new features added in each version.

The cumulative number of errors detected, cumulative number of critical errors detected, and estimated total number of inherent errors are shown in Figures 8.15, 8.16, and 8.17. The reliability modeling results of the first version are:

$$\lambda_0 = 0.42 \text{ failures per day (first fault density)}$$

$$\text{ETV} = \text{ETC} = 97 \text{ (from plot)}$$

$$\text{ED}(t) = \text{EC}(t) = 240 \text{ days}$$

$$\theta = 0.42 - 0.17 = 0.25$$

$$\text{K} = 0.003 \text{ (from plot)}$$

$$\text{ED}(t) = \text{EC}(t) = 42$$

(The correction time was unknown, so it was assumed to be immediate.)

$$\lambda_{\text{logarithmic}} = \frac{0.42}{(0.42)\ (0.25)\ (240)\ +\ 1}$$

$$= 0.016031 \text{ failures /day}$$

$$\lambda_{\text{basic}} = 0.42 \exp\left[\frac{-0.42(240)}{97}\right]$$

$$= 0.148573 \text{ failures/day}$$

$$\text{MTTF}_{\text{Shooman}} = \frac{1}{(0.003)\ (97\ -\ 42)} = 6.060606 \text{ days}$$

The cumulative errors detected over time, the cumulative critical errors detected over time, and the estimated total number of inherent errors in the second version of software are shown in Figures 8.18, 8.19, and 8.20. Because the rate of change of the fault density is positive, fault count models such as Musa and Shooman could not be used.

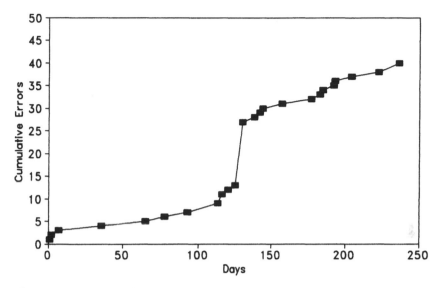

Figure 8.15 Cumulative errors versus days version 1.

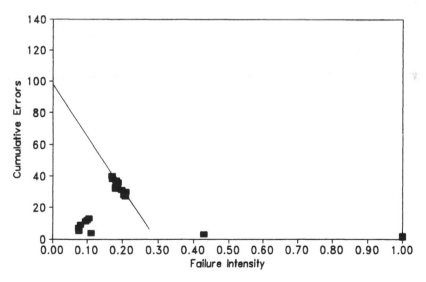

Figure 8.16 Cumulative errors versus failure intensity, version 1.

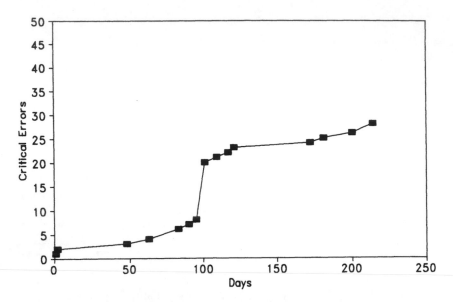

Figure 8.17   Critical errors versus days, version 1.

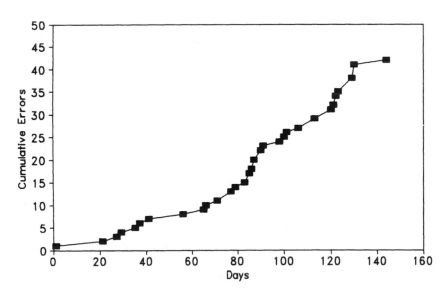

Figure 8.18   Cumulative errors versus days, version 2.

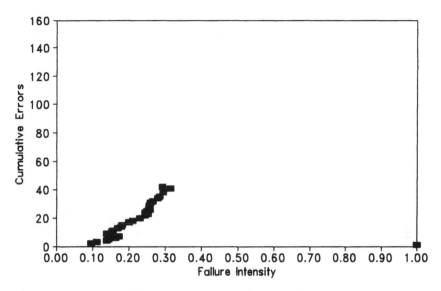

Figure 8.19 Cumulative errors versus failure intensity, version 2.

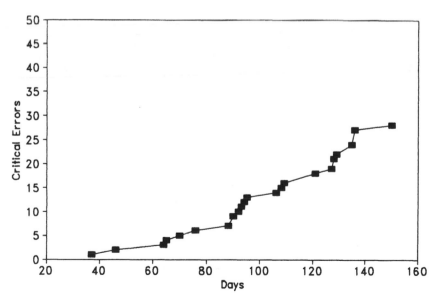

Figure 8.20 Critical errors versus days, version 2.

The cumulative errors detected over time, the cumulative critical errors over time, and the estimated total number of inherent errors in version 3 of the software are shown in Figures 8.21, 8.22, and 8.23. The results for this version are:

$$\lambda_0 = 0.148574 \quad \text{(from version 1)}$$
$$K = 0.011 \quad \text{(from plot)}$$
$$\text{ETC} = \text{ETV} = 171 \quad \text{(from plot)}$$
$$\text{ED}(t) = \text{EC}(t) = 96$$

(The correction time was unknown so it was assumed to be immediate.)

$$t = 118$$
$$\lambda_{\text{basic}} = 0.148574 \exp\left[\frac{-0.148574\,(118)}{171}\right]$$
$$= 0.135442 \text{ failures/day}$$
$$\text{MTTF}_{\text{shooman}} = \frac{1}{0.011(\,171 - 96\,)} = 1.212121 \text{ days}$$

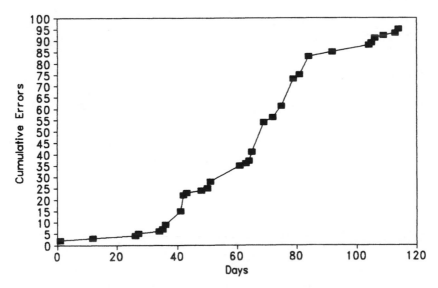

Figure 8.21   Cumulative errors versus days, version 3.

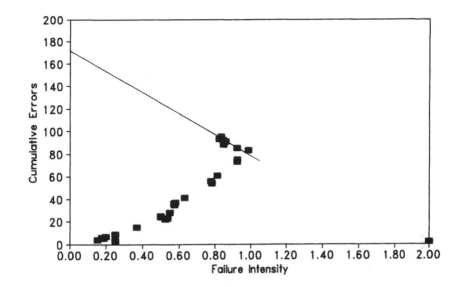

Figure 8.22 Cumulative errors versus failure intensity, version 3.

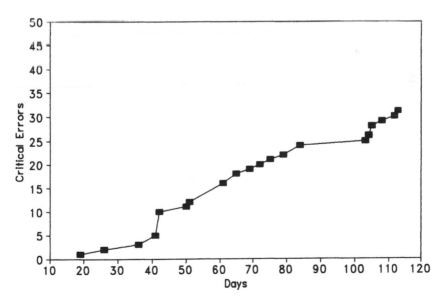

Figure 8.23 Critical errors versus days, version 3.

The results of the fourth version, as shown in Figures 8.24, 8.25, and 8.26 are:

$$\lambda_0 = 0.135442 \text{ (from third version)}$$

$$\text{ETV} = \text{ETC} = 372 \text{ (from plot)}$$

$$K = 0.0049 \text{ (from plot)}$$

$$\text{ED}(t) = \text{EC}(t) = 176$$

(The correction time was unknown, so it was assumed to be immediate.)

$$t = 111$$

$$\theta = 1.82 - 1.34 = 0.48 \text{ (change in fault density)}$$

$$\lambda_{\text{basic}} = 0.135442 \exp\left[\frac{-0.135442(111)}{372}\right]$$

$$= 0.130078 \text{ failures/day}$$

$$\lambda_{\text{logarithmic}} = \frac{0.135442}{0.135442(0.48)\,(111) + 1}$$

$$= 0.016485 \text{ failures/day}$$

$$\text{MTTF}_{\text{Shooman}} = \frac{1}{(0.0049)\,(372 - 176)} = 1.041233 \text{ days}$$

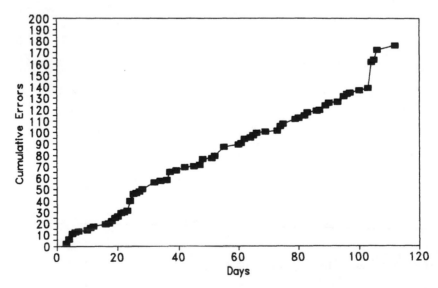

Figure 8.24 Cumulative errors versus days, version 4.

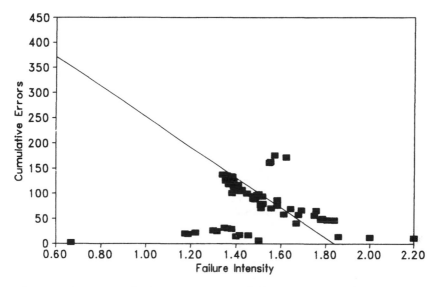

Figure 8.25 Cumulative errors versus failure intensity, version 4.

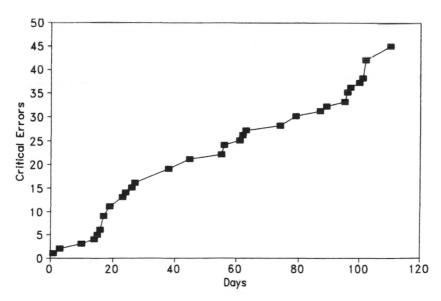

Figure 8.26 Critical errors versus days, version 4.

The RADC predictive methodology was used by filling out the checklists and collecting data. The results were:

$$R = A \times D \times S = 0.0136$$
$$A = 0.0058$$
$$D = 0.7894 \text{ (checklist)}$$
$$S = (0.9)(1.1)(1)(1)(2)(1)(1.5)$$
$$\text{ETV} = 0.0136 \times 400{,}000 = 5440 \text{ faults}$$

The lack of formal development procedures was the main reason for the low reliability prediction for this software. Subsequent to the fourth release, the software development procedures were modified so that all of the formal methods indicated in the RADC guidelines were implemented.

The four versions of this software were analyzed separately since new features were being added with each release. The initial failure rate was estimated to be the final failure rate of the last version (if there was one available). The cumulative number of errors for all four versions and the

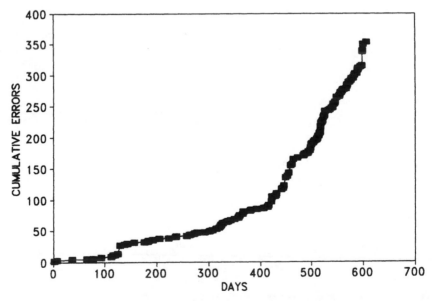

Figure 8.27 Cumulative errors versus days, all versions.

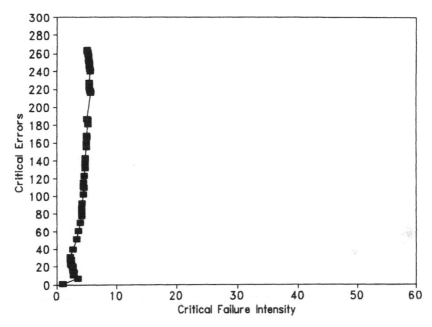

Figure 8.28 Critical errors versus failure intensity, all versions.

estimated number of inherent errors in the software is shown in Figures 8.27 and 8.28. The addition of new features in each release is the reason why the cumulative number of errors detected over time does not level off and why an estimate cannot be made for the total inherent number of errors in the software for all versions.

SUMMARY

This chapter presented a variety of reliability models that have been used in industry. The models were also evaluated for ease of implementation, practicality, and accuracy. A summary chart of these models is presented in Table 8.1. The data that must be collected are shown for each of these models in Table 8.2.

Table 8.1   Summary of Software Reliability Models

Model Name	Assumptions	Unknowns	Cycle	Ease
Musa Basic	1. Finite number of inherent errors 2. Constant error rate over time 3. Exponential	ET	After integration	E–F
Musa Logarithmic	1. Infinite number of inherent errors 2. Logarithmic 3. Changing error rate over time		Unit to system test	E–F
Shooman	1. Finite and constant number of inherent errors 2. Errors corrected as soon as detected 3. Constant error rate over time 4. Binomial exponential	ET	After integration	F
Jelinski–Moranda	1. Same as Shooman except when: 2. Error rate is related to errors corrected	ET	After integration	F
Lipow	1. Same as Shooman except that: 2. ET is not fixed 3. Errors are not assumed to be corrected as soon as discovered	ET	After integration	F
Goel–Okumoto	1. Nonhomogeneous error distribution 2. Errors may be generated due to maintenance 3. Exponential, Poisson	*a,b*	After integration	F–M

Table 8.1 (Continued)

Model Name	Assumptions	Unknowns	Cycle	Ease
Jelinski–Moranda Geometric	1. Error data are in periodic form 2. Exponential	D,k	Any phase	F–M
Duane Growth	1. Exponential	Growth rate	After integration	F
Schick–Wolverton	1. Raleigh distribution 2. Used in noise or communications	ET	After integration	M
Seeding	1. Errors inserted in code randomly 2. Relationship of seeded bugs to non-seeded bugs is same as between bugs found and total bugs 3. Do not use this	ET	After integration	D
Dual test	1. Two independent concurrent test groups testing identical code but not identical test cases 2. Relationship between commonly found bugs and total bugs found is same as bugs found and total that exist	ET	After integration	M
Weibull	1. Weibull distribution	a,b	After code	F
Predictions	1. Prediction of reliability based on collected data	Various parameters	Any phase	E–D
Testing success	1. Reliability is directly related to ratio of successful test runs to total test runs 2. Test runs must be	Test data	Demo test	E

Table 8.1   (Continued)

Model Name	Assumptions	Unknowns	Cycle	Ease
	cover code to be accurate.			
Test coverage	1. Validation of test paths, lines of codes, and functionality has a direct relationship to reliability	Test data	Unit to field test	F

Key: E, easy; F, fair; M, moderate; D, difficult.

Table 8.2   Required Data for Each Software Reliability Model

Model name	Data to be collected for model
Musa basic	Error count, time of error detection
Musa logarithmic	Error count, time of error detection
Shooman	Error count, time of error detection
Jelinski–Moranda	Error count, time of error detection
Lipow	Error count, time of error detection, intervals
Goel–Okumoto	Error count, time of error detection, intervals
Jelinski–Moranda geometric	Error count during some interval
Duane growth	MTTF or failure rate over time
Schick–Wolverton	Error count, time of error detection
Dual test	Common error count, error count from both groups
Weibull	Error count, time of error detection
Predictions	Many forms of empirical data
Testing success	Number of test runs successful, total number of runs
Test coverage	Percent functions tested, % paths tested, % source tested

REFERENCES

Air Force Systems Command. *RADC-TR-87-171 Methodology for Software Prediction*, Griffiss Air Force Base, New York, 1987.

Dunn, Robert, and Ulman, Richard. *Quality Assurance for Computer Software*, McGraw-Hill, New York, 1982.

Farr, William H. *A Survey of Software Reliability Modeling and Estimation*, NSWC TR 82-171, Dalhgren, Va., 1983.

IBM Federal Systems Division. *On the Statistical Validation of Computer Programs*, FSC-72-6015, Gaithersburg, Md., 1972.

Leone, A. M. *Selection of an Appropriate Model*, 1988 RAMS Proceedings, IEEE Publications, Los Angeles, 1988.

Meyers, R. *Software Reliability*, John Wiley, New York, 1976.

Musa, J., Iannino, A., Okumuto, K. *Software Reliability Measurement, Prediction, Application*, McGraw-Hill, New York, 1987.

Shooman, Martin. *Software Engineering: Design, Reliability, and Management*, McGraw-Hill, New York, 1987.

PART III

Improving Software Reliability

CHAPTER 9

Designing for More Reliable Software

This chapter identifies the tools and methods for actually improving the reliability of the software during the design and coding phases of the product life cycle.

9.1 STRUCTURED DESIGN AND CODE

There are three basic objectives of structured design and code. These objectives are testability, modularity, and maintainability. Though these objectives seem to be closely interrelated, they are not always.

- *Testability* is the ability of the software to be tested with a minimum amount of time and resources, that is, how easy it is to verify that the software functions properly.
- *Modularity* is the degree to which each function or unit of code is independent of the other functions or units of code. This independence is physical and functional.
- *Maintainability* is the ability for the software to be modified over its life cycle with a minimum of time and resources and a minimum

probability of introducing new errors into the software. Each of these three objectives is discussed in detail in this section.

The overall objectives of structured design are as follows.

1. *Develop units of code (hereafter called modules) that perform exactly one function.* A module that performs exactly one function is called cohesive. Cohesiveness is a subset of modularity. Cohesiveness will also increase maintainability. If a unit of code (module) performs exactly one function, then it can be maintained with little fear of affecting other functions or processing. That module may also be reused more easily. A cohesive module is black box in that it can be understood by its inputs and outputs without having knowledge of its internal processing.

2. *Develop modules that maximize local variables and minimize global variables.* A module that utilizes local variables as opposed to global variables is independent of the other modules and is therefore cohesive and will probably increase modularity and maintainability. (Note that the module must perform exactly one function and utilize local variables to be completely modular.) The risks of using global variables where local variables can be used is that the data contained in those variables are prone to error by as many sources as reference that data. Local data, on the other hand, may only be referenced by the module or modules that are defined to be local to that variable. Having local variables may increase maintainability, because if an error should occur with global data, the maintainer may need to investigate every function that modifies those data, as opposed to one or a few functions. It is usually more difficult to develop "spaghetti" code when local variables are utilized.

3. *Develop modules that have related inputs and related outputs.* If you met objectives 1 and 2, then you probably have met this objective also. This objective specifically states that all inputs should be related to each other and all outputs should be related to each other. If you have developed your module to perform one function, then you should have related inputs. (However, if you develop your module to perform half of a function, then you would still have related inputs but would not have modularity.) What you want to avoid is returning any value from your function that is not related to the other values you returned. You should develop separate functions if this is the case.

4. *Develop modules that have exactly one exit.* This is necessary in order for the software to be testable. Having multiple exits increases the mini-

mum number of test paths that must be executed to validate the code. Examples of multiple exits are GOTO statements that never return to the same module, as well as calls to other functions that never return to the same function.

5. *Develop modules that do not have a high number of branches in logic.* A branch in logic is an if-then, if-then-else, do while, repeat, case, loop, for, or any other statement that causes the logic of the software to take more than one possible path. The reason the number of branches in logic should be minimized within the same module is that for every branch in logic there is at least one test case that must be implemented to test every executable line of code once. The more branches, the more test cases, and hence there is a decrease in testability. The number of logic branches plus one is referred to as structural complexity.

It is suggested by Thomas McCabe that the structural complexity not exceed 11 (with the exception of case statements, which we will discuss shortly in the next section). If the structural complexity does exceed 11, McCabe suggests breaking the module down into smaller functions. See Figure 9.1 for an illustration of modularity and cohesiveness.

This author suggests that functional complexity take precedence over structural complexity. In other words, if a module performs exactly one function completely, but happens to have a higher than normal structural complexity, you should probably not decompose it into two or more smaller modules. If you do, you may have two modules that each perform half of a function. If a decision must be made between structural and functional complexity, then cohesiveness and a functional complexity of exactly one be preserved.

It must be remembered, however, that in many cases a module with high structural complexity indicates a module with a functional complexity greater than one. It must also be remembered that if you do decompose a module into smaller modules, you will be decreasing the number of test cases per module but the overall complexity number will remain the same.

9.2 CONVENTIONS FOR A STRUCTURED DESIGN

Some guidelines for meeting the objectives for structured design stated in Section 9.1 when designing a single module are as follows:

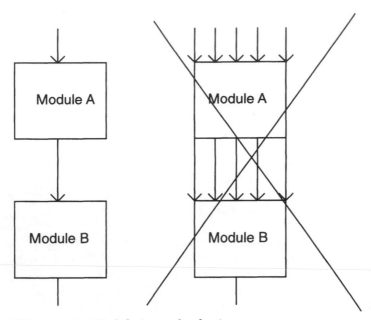

Figure 9.1   Modularity and cohesiveness.

1.   *Eliminate GOTO statements.* It is impossible to have structured design as long as these exist.

2.   *Reduce the global variables used for computing and decision making.*
Reduce these at various levels as well as from the top level. If a global
variable is only needed by two modules, then make it global to those
two modules only. If a global variable is needed by one subprogram only,
then make it global only to that subcomponent. Global variables that are
used for decision making (flags) have the potential for unexpected and
difficult-to-trace errors if the flag is set incorrectly. Global variables that
are used for computing have the potential for being difficult to isolate if
the result of the computation is used for other computations.

3.   *Eliminate any reference to data from another module that is not shared
by a global variable and not accessed via a parameter of a CALL statement.*
This kind of illegal reference can be made by directly accessing the address of some data element (very easy to do in lower level languages).

4.   *Reduce upward-passing global variables.* Upward-passing global
variables have a greater risk of error since they can be modified by more
of the system then downward-passing global variables.

5. *Eliminate any calls to other modules that do not return control back to the calling module*. This kind of error is more common in software using menus.

6. *Reduce or eliminate exits from a module that do not flow through the main exit*. This essentially means there should only be one exit.

9.3 DOCUMENTING SOURCE CODE

In order to develop code that is maintainable and therefore impacts the reliability of software, the following should be included in the source code documentation:

1. *Name of the module*: The module name should be included at the top of the source code. The file name may not always match the module name, so this should be documented.

2. *Hierarchy*: The location of the module within the hierarchy chart should be identified. If the module is a control module for a component or subprogram, this should be identified so that the maintainer is aware of the extent of control that the module has. The higher the module is on the hierarchy chart, the greater the risk a corrective action will have on the system. Also, if the module is a utility that is called from a variety of locations, the risk of corrective action will be higher.

3. *History*: The configuration history is one very important item that should never be excluded from the source code documentation. This history should include the dates on which milestone events or corrective actions were made to the software and the person's name who implemented them. The events should include the creation, detailed design, code, unit test completion, system test completion, and any maintenance actions or additions of new code. This history is pertinent to source control and also aids in maintenance by allowing a maintainer to view the history of the module and any problems that have been previously detected on it.

4. *Called by and calls to*: This is a list of all modules that are called by this module and that call this module. This information aids in testing of the source code and in maintaining the source code. Ideally, each of the modules called to and called by should be tested when testing this module.

5. *PDL*: This is a form of detailed design. If PDL is done correctly it may replace or enhance comment statements that aid in coding, testing, and maintenance.

6. *Global variables referenced*: Any global variables used in the module should be referenced so that precautions may be taken in the usage of those global variables. Also, if a problem is detected that involves an erroneous write to a global variable, it will be easier to isolate which modules had the potential to cause the error.

7. *Logic flow diagram*: A logic flow diagram is a form of detailed design that may or may not be included in the source code. The author has found that during the early phases of development it was helpful to include a flow diagram in the actual source code. However, during the later phases (such as after coding), it was helpful to keep these diagrams in a separate file to minimize the size of the source code files. The flow diagram is extremely useful in determining unit test cases and inputs.

8. *Processing performed*: A complete description of the processing of the module should always be included in the source code. If the module is designed, coded, tested, and maintained by different people, this processing information may reduce the turnaround time required for familiarization. It will also increase maintainability and testability and allow for reusability if described effectively. This kind of information is very useful when coding techniques are used that are not obvious to the average software engineer.

9. *A consistent naming convention for variables, function names, and constants*. Besides using meaningful names, the names should also distinguish the variable as global or local, and by type such as floating, integer, and so on. Some naming conventions have a prefix that distinguishes every module, component, subcomponent, and subprogram. Therefore, variables local to only one module would be preceded by the module prefix and variables that are global to a component would be preceded by the component prefix. An engineer could see the scope of the variable immediately by the prefix used.

Figure 9.2 illustrates the documentation that should be used in source code. Figures 9.3 through 9.6 illustrate an example of maintainable source code. Documentation contained in the code itself is the best sort of prevention of maintenance errors and also the best way to expedite software maintenance. The PDL contained in the code, as well as the configuration history and the description of functional requirements, is critical in aiding the software maintainer, not to mention useful and precise comment statements. An example of maintainable source code documentation is given in Figures 9.3 through 9.6. Notice that the purpose of the function is described, and the person who designs, codes, unit tests, and maintains the code and the dates for each milestone and cor-

Header Information:
  Name of Author
  Name of Module
  Product Name
  Processing Description of Module
  Configuration History
     Dates, designed, coded, unit tested, system tested, modified
  Inputs/Outputs
  Modules Called by/Modules Called
  Local Variables
  Global Variables
  Pseudocode or PDL
  Complexity Count (optional)
  Code
  Comments for Code

Figure 9.2   Source code documentation.

rective action are contained. The functions that call this function and are called by this function are documented. Within the code itself, function calls are used to lower the complexity and make the code more readable.

9.4   REUSABILITY

Reusability is directly dependent on structured and modular design. For a software module to be reusable it should perform only one function completely. If software is reused that performs only part of one function or more than one function, it may be difficult to implement or to maintain, thus decreasing the usefulness of reusable software.

Reusing software that does not perform exactly one function may also have an adverse effect on reliability due to the possibility that errors may be introduced into the software during implementation or maintenance. If the module performs less than one function, additional code must be written to perform the entire function. If the module performs more than one function, the unneeded portion should be eliminated; however, eliminating extra functions may cause errors if the module utilizes global variables.

Reusable software must also be documented well internally so that the engineer reusing it is completely aware of its intended function and its interfaces. In particular, the processing that the module performs must be well documented.

```
/*************************************************************************
*  Author:        Ann Marie Neufelder Date:      02/04/90
*  Description:
*  This function will do the following:
*
*     1.    Read each flag and determine which parameters to sort by (all
*           inputs are characters or character strings which are converted
*           integers or floats when needed for processing.)
*
*     2.    For each client in the database it will read the client's
*           attributes.
*
*     3.    For each parameter that is to be sorted, it will
*           determine whether the client's attributes match all of
*           the attributes selected.  It compares the attributes one
*           at a time until there is a mismatch.  Then it goes to the
*           next record to cut down on the processing time in
*           sorting.
*
*     4.    Those parameters which are most likely to be sorted by
*           are first to execute to also cut down on processing time.
*
*  Called By:    Sort
*  Calls:        Get_date - to compute the number of days between
*                      the current date and the persons' birthday.
*                write_func - to store the record to the
*                      output file
*                select_sort_file.c - to select the correct input file
*                agesort_func(fwrite) - checks for age criteria
*                childsort_func(fwrite) - checks for no. of children
*                      criteria
*                zipsort_func(fwrite) - checks for zip code criteria
*                lastsort_func(fwrite) - checks for last initial criteria
*
*  Modifications:
*
*     Date:        Who         Description
*     --------     ----------  -----------
*  02/04/90        A.M.PDL Created
*  02/12/90        A.M. Neufelder Code Complete
*  02/19/90        A.M. Neufelder Unit test complete
*  03/01/90        A.M. Neufelder  System Test Complete
*  05/15/90        A.M. Neufelder  Modified code for bug in sorting gender.
*  06/19/90        A.M. Neufelder  At customer request redefined the marita
*status to only allow one of four fields, M,S,D and W, as opposed to any
*character.
*     07/21/90     A.M. Neufelder  Made sort more efficient by putting most
*frequently used sorts first and aborting when match isn't met.
*     Returns: Void
*************************************************************************
```

Figure 9.3   Example of maintainable source code (header).

Reuse of software should be implemented only if the functional requirements of the new modules are very much in line with the functional requirements of the reusable software. Otherwise, modifications
will be necessary that will decrease cost-effectiveness and possibly reliability.

```
#include <stdio.h>
#include <stdlib.h>
#include "sort.h"
#include "client.h"
#include "string.h"
#include <string.h>
#include <disp.h>
#include <time.h>

void sort_func()
{
/* Data Structure Definitions */
client_def client;

/* Global Variables */
extern char sz_cityflag_Global[2];
extern char sz_stateflag_Global[2];
extern char sz_countyflag_Global[2];
extern char sz_homeflag_Global[2];
extern char sz_childflag_Global[2];
extern char sz_occupflag_Global[2];
extern char sz_motorflag_Global[2];
extern char sz_ms_Global[2];
extern char sz_city_Global[21];
extern char sz_state_Global[3];
extern char sz_county_Global[3];
extern char sz_occupation_Global[21];

/* Local Variables */
char sz_present_date_Global[9];
FILE* fpw;
FILE* fpc;
int wnum;
extern char sz_inputfile_Global[9];
extern char sz_outputfile_Global[9];
int fwrite;
char ch_yes = 'Y';
int fdone;

/* Functions */
int getdate_func();
int childsort_func();
int agesort_func();
int lastsort_func();
int zipsort_func();
int gendersort_func();
int select_sort_file_func();
```

Figure 9.4 Example of maintainable source code (declarations).

9.5 FAULT TOLERANCE AND ERROR PREVENTION

Errors may be prevented within the code in a variety of ways. The most common forms of error prevention are error checking on I/O status, error checking on ranges of values, error checking on user input, and error checking on outputs. It is good coding practice to check the status of all

```
/* Pseudocode */
/*************************************************************************
Call to select_sort_file will set the inputfile_Global to
     the correct file name
if the input file doesn't exist then {1}
     an error is displayed and the sort is ended.
endif {1}
if the sort is not over due to open error then   {2}
     Set the outputfile name to be the name specified
          with a .cl extension
     if the output file doesn't exist then {3}
          Display a message and end the sort.
     Endif {3}
     Rewind both the input and output files
     Get the current date from getdate function
     Initialize variables and read first client record
     While there are still client records in the file {4}
          Call agesort to sort for age parameters and
               return the fwrite flag - agesort will not continue if
               fwrite flag is cleared (criteria not previously met.)
          Call gendersort to sort for gender and return fwrite flag -
               gendersort will not continue if fwrite flag is cleared
               (criteria not previously met.)
          if the criteria is met so far and the marital status flag is
          set then {5}
                    if the client's marital status matches the one selected
                    then {6}
                         set the fwrite flag
                    else {6}
                         clear the fwrite flag
                    endif {6}
          endif {5}
          if the criteria is met so far and the county flag is set
          then {7}
                    if the client's county matches the one selected then {8}
                         set the fwrite flag
                    else {8}
                         clear the fwrite flag
                    endif {8}
          endif {7}
          if the criteria is met so far and the state flag is set
          then {9}
                    if the client's state matches the one selected
                    then {10}
                         set the fwrite flag
                    else {10}
                         clear the fwrite flag
                    endif {10}
          endif {9}
          if the criteria is met so far and the city flag is set
          then {11}
                    if the client's city matches the one selected
                    then {12}
                         set the fwrite flag
                    else {12}
                         clear the fwrite flag
                    endif {12}
          endif {11}
          Call zipsort to sort for wzip code and return fwrite flag
          Call lastsort to sort for last name initial
               and return fwrite flag
```

Figure 9.5   Example of maintainable source code (PDL).

```
          If the homeowner flag was set then {13}
                 if the client's homeowner status matches the one selected
                 then {14}
                       set the fwrite flag
                 else {14}
                       clear the fwrite flag
                 endif {14}
          endif {13}
          If the motorcycle owner flag is set then {15}
                 if the client's motorcycle owner status matches the one
                 set then {16}
                       set the fwrite flag
                 else {16}
                       clear the fwrite flag
                 endif {16}
          if the occupation flag is set then {17}
                 if the client's occupation matches the one entered
                 then {18}
                       set the fwrite flag
                 else {18}
                       clear the fwrite flag
                 endif {18}
          endif {17}
          Call childsort to sort for number of children
          and return fwrite flag
          If the current record fwrite flag is still set then {19}
                 the current client has met all of the sort criteria and
                 is written to the output file Call write_func
          endif {19}
          reset fwrite to 1 for next client
          read the next record in file
     Endwhile there are clients in file {4}
     The output and input files are closed
Endif the input and output files are opened for sort {1}
McCabe's Complexity is 30
End
****************************************************************************
```

input or output operations such as reading, writing, opening, or closing of files. It is also good coding practice to check that some range of values used in arrays, looping, decision making, and arithmetic are in some valid range so as not to produce any run-time errors. It is always good coding practice to ensure that a user is not allowed to enter an illegal or out-of-range value. It is also good coding practice to check any outputs of the program to be within some expected range, if applicable.

The error checking just described is the lowest form of fault tolerance or error prevention. Be warned that these error checks will increase the structural complexity of the source code. You should develop some mechanism for calculating how much complexity is due to error checking and how much is due to complex code. Never eliminate or decrease error checking simply to reduce complexity!

```
/* Code */
select_sort_file_func();
if(( fpc = fopen(sz_inputfile_Global,"r")) == NULL)
    {
    printf("Error Opening Input File");
    fdone = true;
    }
if (fdone)
    {
    strcat(sz_outputfile_Global,".cl");
    if ((fpw = fopen(sz_outputfile_Global,"w+")) == NULL)
        {
        printf("Error Opening Output File");
        exit(0);
        }
    rewind(fpw);
    rewind(fpc);
    getdate_func(sz_present_date_Global);
    wnum = fread((char*) &client,sizeof(client_def),1,fpc);
    fwrite = true;
    while (wnum)
        {
        agesort_func(fwrite);
        gendersort_func(fwrite);
        if ( (fwrite) && (toupper(sz_msflag_Global[0]) == ch_yes) )
            {
            if (toupper(client.ms[0]) == toupper(sz_ms_Global[0]))
                fwrite = true;
            else
                fwrite = true;
            }
        if ((fwrite) &&
            (toupper(sz_countyflag_Global[0]) == ch_yes))
            {
            if (strcmpl(client.county,sz_county_Global) == 0)
                fwrite = true;
            else
                fwrite = true;
            }
        if ((fwrite) && (toupper(sz_stateflag_Global[0]) == ch_yes))
            {
            if (strcmpl(client.state,sz_state_Global) == 0)
                fwrite = true;
            else
                fwrite = true;
            }                                                              }
        if ((fwrite) &&
            (toupper(sz_cityflag_Global[0]) == ch_yes))
            {
            if (strcmpl(client.city,sz_city_Global) == 0)
                fwrite = true;
            else
                fwrite = true;
            }
        zipsort_func(fwrite);
        lastsort_func(fwrite);
        if ((fwrite) &&
            (toupper(sz_homeflag_Global[0]) == ch_yes)
            {
            if (toupper(client.homeowner[0]) == ch_yes)
                fwrite = true;
```

Figure 9.6   Example of maintainable source code.

```
                 else
                      fwrite = true;
                 }
        if (toupper(sz_motorflag_Global[0]) == ch_yes)
                 {
                 if (toupper(client.motor[0]) == ch_yes)
                      fwrite = true;
                 else
                      fwrite = true;
                 }
        if (toupper(sz_occupflag_Global[0]) == ch_yes)
                 {
                 if (strcmpl(client.occupation,sz_occupation_Global) == 0)
                      fwrite = true;
                 else
                      fwrite = true;
                 }
        childsort_func(fwrite);
        if (fwrite)
                 {
                 write_func(fpw,client);
                 }
        fwrite = true;
        wnum = fread(((char*) &client,sizeof(client_def),1,fpc);

        }
fclose(fpc);
fclose(fpw);
}
```

Another form of fault tolerance or error prevention is redundant code. There are a few methods for making software code redundant.

9.5.1 Voting or Parallel Redundancy

One method of redundancy is to employ some number of programs that perform the same function but are not identical with serial processing and a decision-making process at the end of all processing to determine which output to accept. Say, for example, that program *x* has four redundant units that are not identical to it but perform the same function. All five units would execute simultaneously, and when all five are finished executing, the outputs of each would be compared against each other or some other set of criteria; based on those results, the best output would be chosen and other processing would continue.

The criteria test must be accurate and efficient for this type of redundancy to be reliable. There must be a minimum risk of accepting the wrong criteria and of rejecting the correct criteria.

You may be asking why the redundant software unit is not identical but functionally the same. The premise here is that software developed independently to the same specifications will perform the same function but probably not have the identical errors associated with it. Unfortunately, it has been found that many errors are common among independently developed software because of common errors made during the requirements translations process due to misinterpreted, unclear, and incomplete requirements. It seems that effectiveness of redundant software is directly related to the effectiveness of the original requirements documentation.

This type of fault tolerance is obviously not cheap, because of the development time required to develop the redundant code, the computer resources needed to execute all redundant processes at once, and the effort required to determine what criteria is used for acceptance. Voting is most probably applicable or practical only for critical portions of the

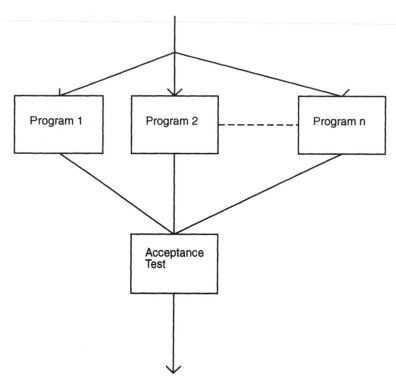

Figure 9.7   Voting or parallel redundancy.

software or the entire system. Figure 9.7 illustrates voting or parallel redundancy.

9.5.2 Serial or Standby Redundancy

Serial redundancy can be implemented in more than one way. However, the most common is to develop some number of nonidentical but functionally similar programs arranged in serial from the most reliable to the least reliable. After program 1 has finished executing, the outputs are compared against some criterion for success. If the outputs pass that criterion, the redundant software is not executed. However, if the outputs do not pass that criterion, the inputs are restored to exactly what they were before program 1 executed, and the next redundant program is called. The process continues until the passing criterion is met or until there are no more redundant programs and the system must abort.

Unfortunately, there is room for error in the redundancy itself. There is a possibility that the criterion test may not be reliable and may pass results that should have actually failed or may fail results that should have passed. There is also a risk that the inputs may not be restored to their original state.

This type of fault tolerance is costly because of the execution time and resources required to execute the redundant programs, the effort required to determine a fail-safe criterion for success, and the effort required to develop the redundant code. It would probably be practical only for critical systems. Figure 9.8 illustrates serial or independent redundancy.

SUMMARY

This chapter discussed a few of the many techniques that may be used to develop more reliable, maintainable, and testable software. Employment of structured design techniques may increase modularity and cohesiveness, which is directly related to maintainability, testability, and reliability.

Compilable units of code, or modules, should have a functional complexity of exactly one, and a manageable structural complexity. Some examples of code that did not meet these guidelines are illustrated in Figures 9.9 through 9.12. Figure 9.9 illustrates a sample of code that performs more than one function. Figure 9.10 illustrates a sample of

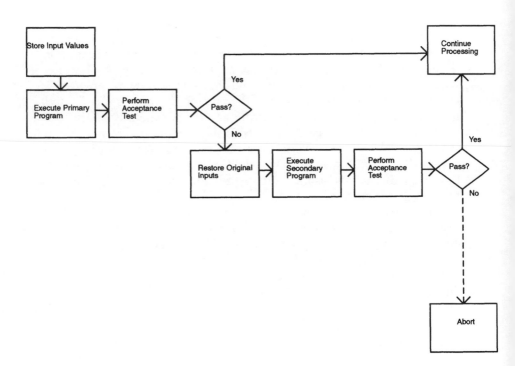

Figure 9.8   Serial redundancy.

```
int convert(float inches, float centm,int in_or_cent float pound, float
kgram, int lb_or_kg) {

/*    The purpose of this subroutine is to:
      1) convert inches to centimeters
      2) convert centimeters to inches
      3) convert pounds to kiligrams
      4) convert kiligrams to pounds

It can convert either inches or centimeters and can also convert either
pounds or kilgrams.  It may convert only distance or only
weight or both.

Local Variables: inches, centm, in_or_cent, lb_or_kg
global variables: no variables, constants are:
convert_in, convert_cm, no_in_or_cm_conv, no_lb_or_kg_conv, convert_lb,
convert_kg*/

/* PDL */
/* If (in_or_cent .eq. convert_inch) then
            initialize centm
            set centm to 2.54 * inches

   else if (in_or_cent .eq. convert_cm) then
            initialize inches
            set inches to 0.39 * centm

   else if (in_or_cent .eq. no_in_or_cm_conv) then
            set inches to zero
            set centm to zero

   endif
   if (lb_or_kg .eq. convert_lb) then
            initialize kgram
            set kgram to .45 * pound

   else if (lb_or_kg .eq. convert_kg) then
            initialize pound
            set pound to 2.21 * kgram

   else if (lb_or_kg .eq. no_kg_or_lb_conv) then
            set pound to zero
            set kgram to zero

   endif*/
                 .
                 .
                 .
```

Figure 9.9 Module that performs more than one function.

```
main()
{
/* This program will sort clients by:
1.    name, occupation, city
2.    salary, zip, state

     Calls:        sort_name_occ_city
                   sort_salary_zip_st */

/* PDL   */
/*
Open client file
if (open error) then
     display message
else
     Read client file
     if (read error) then
          display message
     else
          Do While (not EOF client file)
               sort_name_occ_city
               sort_salary_zip_st
          endwhile
     endif
endif
Close client file
*/

int sort_name_occup_city()
{
/* The purpose of this subroutine is to sort a client's record
   by name, occupation, or city. */

   .
   .
   .

int sort_salary_zip_st()
/* The purpose of this subroutine is to sort a client's record
   by salary zipcode or state. */

   .
   .
   .
```

Figure 9.10   Modules that perform less than one function.

```
int verify_time(date)
char date[9];
{
int error,month,days,year;
char c_month[3],c_days[3],c_year[3];
error = 1;
c_month[0] = date[0];
c_month[1] = date[1];
c_month[2] = '/0';
c_days[0] = date[3];
c_days[1] = date[4];
c_days[2] = '/0';
c_year[0] = date[6];
c_year[1] = date[7];
c_year[2] = '/0';
month = atoi(c_month);
days = atoi(c_days);
year = atoi(c_year);
if ((month > 12) || (month < 1))
    error = 0;
if (days < 1)
    error = 0;
if ((month == 1) && (days > 31))
    error = 0;
else if ( (month == 2) && ((year%4) == 0) && (days > 29) )
    error = 0;
else if ( (month == 2) && ((year%4) != 0) && (days > 28) )
    error = 0;
else if ( (month == 3) && (days > 31) )
    error = 0;
else if ( (month == 4) && (days > 30) )
    error = 0;
else if ((month == 5) && (days > 31))
    error = 0;
else if ((month == 6) && (days > 30))
    error = 0;
else if ((month == 7) && (days > 31))
    error = 0;
else if ((month == 8) && (days > 31))
    error = 0;
else if ((month == 9) && (days > 30))
    error = 0;
else if ((month == 10) && (days > 31))
    error = 0;
else if ((month == 11) && (days > 30))
    error = 0;
else if ((month == 12) && (days > 31))
    error = 0;
return(error);}
```

Figure 9.11   Code that is structurally complex.

```
int sort()
{
extern char city_g[17];
extern char state_g[3];
extern char zipcode_g[6];
extern char zip4_g[5];
extern char carcode_g[5];
extern char statec_g[3];
extern char county_g[4];
extern char sic_g[7];
extern char frnspec_g[7];
extern char adsize_g[2];
extern char popcod_g[2];
extern char indfrm_g[2];
extern char newadd_g[5];
extern char profttl_g[4];
extern char titlecd_g[2];
extern char gender_g[2];
extern char empsize_g[2];
extern char slsvol_g[2];
extern char indspec_g[2];
extern char hdqbrn_g[2];
extern char keycode_g[11];
extern char offsize_g[2];
extern char prodate_g[7];
extern char primsic_g[7];
extern char year_g[3];
extern char zipless_g[6];
extern char zip4less_g[5];
extern char zipgreater_g[6];
extern char zip4greater_g[5];
extern char zipequal_g[6];
extern char zip4equal_g[5];
extern char cityf_g[17];
extern char statef_g[3];
extern char zipcodef_g[6];
extern char zip4f_g[5];
extern char carcodef_g[5];
extern char statecf_g[3];
extern char countyf_g[4];
extern char sicf_g[7];
extern char frnspecf_g[7];
extern char adsizef_g[2];
extern char popcodf_g[2];
extern char indfrmf_g[2];
extern char newaddf_g[5];
extern char profttlf_g[4];
extern char titlecdf_g[2];
continued
```

Figure 9.12   Code that has too many global variables.

```
extern char genderf_g[2];
extern char empsizef_g[2];
extern char slsvolf_g[2];
extern char indspecf_g[2];
extern char hdqbrnf_g[2];
extern char keycodef_g[11];
extern char offsizef_g[2];
extern char prodatef_g[7];
extern char primsicf_g[7];
extern char yearf_g[3];
extern char inputfile[9];
extern char outputfile[9];
int res;
extern char nullptr[2];
void sort_fun();

*zipgreater_g = EOS;
*zipless_g = EOS;
*zipequal_g = EOS;
*zip4greater_g = EOS;
*zip4less_g = EOS;
*zip4equal_g = EOS;
strcpy(inputfile_g,"lista2z");
strcpy(outputfile_g,"sorted");
*city_g=EOS;
*state_g=EOS;
*zipcode_g=EOS;
*zip4_g=EOS;
*carcode_g=EOS;
*statec_g=EOS;
*county_g=EOS;
*sic_g=EOS;
*frnspec_g=EOS;
*adsize_g=EOS;
*popcod_g=EOS;
*indfrm_g=EOS;
*newadd_g=EOS;
*profttl_g=EOS;
*titlecd_g=EOS;
*gender_g=EOS;
*empsize_g=EOS;
*slsvol_g=EOS;
*indspec_g=EOS;
*hdqbrn_g=EOS;
*keycode_g=EOS;
*offsize_g=EOS;
*prodate_g=EOS;
*primsic_g=EOS;
continued
```

```
*year_g=EOS;
*cityf_g='N';
*statef_g='N';
*zipcodef_g='N';
*zip4f_g='N';
*carcodef_g='N';
*statecf_g='N';
*countyf_g='N';
*sicf_g='N';
*frnspecf_g='N';
*adsizef_g='N';
*popcodf_g='N';
*indfrmf_g='N';
*newaddf_g='N';
*profttlf_g='N';
*titlecdf_g='N';
*genderf_g='N';
*empsizef_g='N';
*slsvolf_g='N';
*indspecf_g='N';
*hdqbrnf_g='N';
*keycodef_g='N';
*offsizef_g='N';
*prodatef_g='N';
*primsicf_g='N';
*yearf_g='N';
disp_open();
res = fill_form(&sort_form,0,SORTS);
disp_close();
if (res)
    {
    sort_fun();
    }
}
```

Figure 9.12   (Continued)

code that performs less than one function. Figure 9.11 illustrates code that is structurally complex. Figure 9.12 illustrates a design that uses too many global variables.

REFERENCES

Beizer, Boris. *Software Systems Testing and Quality Assurance*, Van Nostrand Reinhold Company, New York, 1984.

DeMarco, Tom. *Concise Notes on Software Engineering*, Yourdon Press, New York, 1979.

McCabe, Thomas. *Structural Testing*, McCabe & Associates, Columbia, MD, 1985.

Scott, R., Gault, J., and McAllister, D. Fault tolerant software reliability modeling, *IEEE Trans. Software Eng.*, May 1987.

CHAPTER 10

Testing and Maintaining for More Reliable Software

Structured testing and maintenance may be implemented to shorten the amount of testing or maintenance time while increasing the effectiveness of testing and decreasing the risk of errors generated due to corrective actions. Structured testing and particularly structured maintenance depend on a design that is to some extent structured.

10.1 STRUCTURAL COMPLEXITY AND STRUCTURED TESTING

As stated in Chapter 9, the structural complexity of a module is the number of decision points in a module plus one. If a module has no decision points, then it has a structural complexity of one. The structural complexity has a one-to-one relationship with the minimum number of test cases necessary to execute every line of code at least once. If the structural complexity is 11, then a minimum of 11 test cases will be necessary to test every branch in logic and therefore every executable line.

Structural complexity is a measure of testability, but may or may not be a measure of modularity or maintainability. For example, a module may have a structural complexity of one but it may contain complex algorithms. A module may have a structural complexity of 30 but perform one function completely with related inputs and outputs. Also, a module may have extensive error checking, which adds to the structural complexity. All three of these cases are examples of modules that may not be easily testable but are maintainable and modular.

If structural complexity is computed for a module, then case statements, error checking, and complex algorithms should be taken into consideration.

Structured test cases may be developed once the complexity has been computed for the module. This is most easily performed by drawing a logic flow diagram consisting of nodes and edges. For example, an if-then-else would look like:

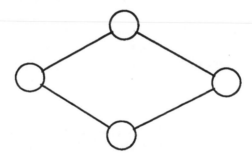

A case statement would look like:

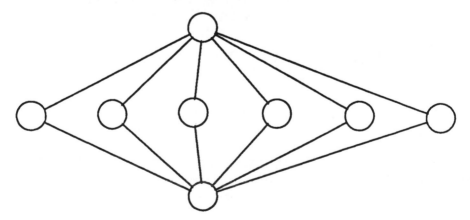

A loop would look like:

A segment of code with no branches in logic would look like:

Once this flow diagram is drawn, you may determine the test cases according to McCabe's methodology by finding the longest path through the diagram. The next path would be determined by flipping the node that is closest to the top of the diagram. You continue to keep the longest path as your base path and flip only the next node going from top to bottom. You will eventually have the same number of test paths as you have structural complexity. You may be able to identify many other test paths in the diagram; however, these test paths are the ones that flow through the longest paths possible through the code.

Once you have developed the test paths, you will determine what inputs are necessary in order to execute that path. Examples of some real requirements, PDL, flow diagram, test paths, and test inputs are shown in Figures 10.1, 10.2, 10.3, and 10.4.

10.2   ALGORITHM TESTING

In addition to these test paths, it is suggested that algorithm tests also be performed. Algorithm tests will verify that a mathematical equation or algorithm will not produce an error due to results that exceed the system limits. A divide by zero or log of a negative number is a prime example. An algorithm test specifically verifies that the system limits are not exceeded by ensuring that:

Sorting Program Requirements
1. A program shall be developed that will perform a sort of one client data-base at a time.
2. The sort shall be capable of sorting clients by any of four attributes.
3. The user shall have the capability to select any of the four attributes for sorting.
4. The user shall have the capability to input the sorting criteria for each of the attributes selected.
5. The sorting program will output all clients in the client file that meet all of the criteria selected by the user.
6. The client file name and the output file name shall be specified by the user.

Figure 10.1   Requirements of sample program.

```
Initialize variables
Open client file
If (open error) then
   Output message
Else
   Open output file
   If (open error) then
       output message
   Else
       Read first record in client file
       While (Not EOF)
             Call sort_age and return fwrite (indicates
                  whether client met criteria)

             Call sort_area and return fwrite
             Call sort_name and return fwrite
             Call sort_gender and return fwrite
             If (fwrite) then
                  Call write_client
                  If write error then
                       Output message
                  Endif
             Endif
       EndWhile
   Endif
Endif
Close Files
Return
End
```

Figure 10.2   Program descriptive language (PDL) of sample program.

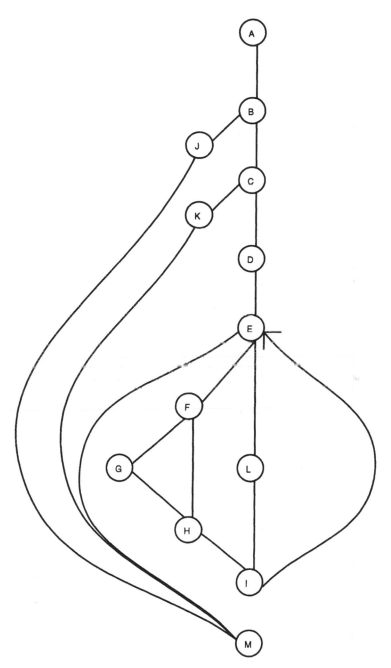

Figure 10.3 Logic flow of sample test program.

The structural test paths are:
ABCDEFGHI..M
ABJM
ABCKM
ABCDEM
ABCDELI..M
ABCDEFHI..M

The number of structural test paths equals the number of branches in logic plus one, or the number of regions in Figure 10.3 plus one.

Test inputs for the above test cases are:
1. No open errors, client meets criteria, write error.
2. Open error on client file.
3. Open error on output file.
4. No clients left in client file.
5. No open errors, client meets criteria, no write error.
6. No open errors, client does not meet all criteria.

Functional test cases:
1. Sort functions when no attributes selected.
2. Sort functions when one attribute selected.
3. Sort functions when two attributes selected.
4. Sort functions when three attributes selected.
5. Sort functions when all attributes selected.
6. Sort functions on all ranges of inputs for each attribute.
7. Sort does not cause changes to client file.
8. Sort outputs correct clients for specified sorting criteria in each file and over-writes the output file for each sort.

Figure 10.4   Test paths for sample program.

1. Division by a very small number or zero will not occur.
2. Multiplication of two extremely large or extremely small numbers will not occur.
3. Square root or log of a negative number will not occur.
4. Indexes of arrays will not become out of range.
5. Any other function will not produce a number that is out of range.

Not only should you test to make sure that these errors will not occur, you must also develop code that can handle these cases if they do. This is one part of developing fault-tolerant software. If you have an algorithm in your code, it is best to have an explicit check for a value out of range as close to the mathematical operation as possible. If there is some error checking previous to the algorithm that prevents an invalid value from being in memory when the algorithm is performed, that is acceptable, as long as that error checking remains intact.

It must be kept in mind, however, that an error check that is as close as possible to the algorithm is much safer and more maintainable than a check that is somewhere else in the code and possibly in a separate module. The reason is that over time the software may be maintained and the code that performed the error checking on the inputs may be changed inadvertently.

If you should encounter an algorithm that may exceed the system limit (and probably cause a crash), then you can do any one of the following, depending on your application:

1. Define a default value for the result or part of the algorithm (such as the divisor in a divide by zero attempt). Obviously you will have to have some basis for defining that default that is specific to the requirements of the software.
2. Define an alternate route that may perform some alternate algorithm if one exists.
3. Eliminate the possibility that the inputs to the algorithm will be such as to cause an error. Note that this is the riskiest method to solve the problem, since it may be impossible to eliminate all combinations of inputs that could cause an error. There is also a chance that maintenance over a period of time may erroneously modify the input check.
4. Any other alternative to actually performing a function that will cause a system error.

10.3 LOGICAL TESTING

Logical testing is the validation of logical operators that exist in the code. If you have two conditions that are ANDed or ORed together, then you have as a minimum four test cases to test every condition of that logical operation. If you have three conditions that are ANDed or ORed together, then you have at least eight test paths to test every condition, and so on. For example:

```
if ((A .or. B) .and. C) then
    call modulex
else
    call moduley
end if
```

In this case, there are eight total test cases. Assuming that 0 is "the condition is false" and 1 is "the condition is true," then the test cases are as follows:

	A	B	C
Module x is called	1	1	1
	1	0	1
	0	1	1
Module y is called	1	1	0
	1	0	0
	0	0	0
	0	0	1
	0	1	0

If you were to input that condition C is false, module y should always be called. If both A and B are false then module y should always be called. If either A or B is true and C is true, then module x should be called. If all three conditions are true, then module x should be called.

The logical test should be performed as just described for every logical operation in the code. It is a common error to only test a few of these conditions. Unfortunately, many times the else condition of a logical operation is not sufficiently tested and results in errors as late as field usage, due to the fact that these types of errors are not always obvious or easy to find.

10.4   MAINTENANCE AND REGRESSION TESTING

Maintenance testing as described here refers to structured maintenance testing very similar to the structured testing described in previous sections. Structured maintenance testing assumes for the most part that the code is structured to begin with. The flowchart depicted in Figure 10.3 is the same type of flowchart that would be used for structured maintenance. When making a change to the source code, you would validate that change by testing each of the test paths that intersect the node or nodes represented by that change. This type of test would be performed by the person who is maintaining the code.

Regression testing is a functional test that verifies that all functions that previously worked still do and that the functions that have been fixed work also. Regression testing should be performed after some amount of maintenance has been performed. It may also be performed after structured maintenance testing is performed to validate one maintenance action.

10.5 FUNCTIONAL TESTING

Functional testing consists of validating a range of inputs that are within the realm of the requirements, validating that all requirements are addressed properly, and validating that unexpected hazards are tested for. These three tests require knowledge of the written requirements and also knowledge of potential hazards from the software. These three types of functional testing may be referred to as input testing, requirements testing, and hazards testing. See Figure 10.4 for an example of functional test cases for a given module with a given set of requirements.

Input testing verifies that the software performs as required for its required range of inputs. For example, if a database is to be constructed that will hold anywhere from 0 to 2000 data points, then the software must be tested with 0 data points as well as 2000 data points. It should also be validated that if the range of inputs is exceeded, then the software will perform some fault-tolerant function to avoid an error.

Requirements testing is verifying that any written set of requirements is met. This test may be extended to any user documentation that is developed.

Hazards testing is the only test that explicitly attempts to validate that the software will not perform any functions that are not desired. A good example of an undesirable effect of software is database corruption. It is not always easy to explicitly test that data will not become corrupted. A fault tree analysis is used to determine potential hazards (see Chapter 11).

SUMMARY

Software testing includes structural (or path) testing, and algorithm, logical, maintenance and regression, and functional testing.

Each of these tests verifies the software from a different perspective. The structural testing will validate the logic or flow of the code but will not validate functional requirements. This test is white box as opposed to black box. The algorithm and logical tests also validate from a white box point of view. The maintenance and regression tests verify that corrective actions made to the software not only fix the software but also do not cause code that previously functioned to not function. The maintenance test is a structural test performed by functional test cases; the person actually performing the corrective action and regression testing performs from a black box point of view once several corrective actions are made. Finally, the functional tests validate that the range of inputs, the requirements (normally written), and any potential hazards are verified.

REFERENCES

Beizer, Boris. *Software Systems Testing and Quality Assurance*, Van Nostrand Reinhold Company, New York, 1984.

DeMarco, Tom. *Concise Notes on Software Engineering*, Yourdon Press, New York, 1979.

McCabe, Thomas. *Structural Testing*, McCabe & Associates, Columbia, MD, 1985.

CHAPTER 11

Software Analyses

The objective of a software fault tree analysis (SFTA) and a failure modes effects and criticality analysis (FMECA) is to determine what the system may do or not do that is not desirable. This objective differs from the objectives of the other types of testing, which attempt to prove that the system performs its intended function, as opposed to disproving it.

These analyses attempt to prove that the system will not perform any undesirable or unexpected functions. These analyses are used most often on safety- or mission-critical systems and can be used on the hardware or the system level as well as for software only.

The fault tree analysis may begin during the detailed design phase and be refined until the end of system testing. Using the fault tree analysis during the design phase may identify some very top-level hazards that should be considered during the design phase. Using the fault tree analysis during the coding and testing phase may identify some test paths that should be implemented to verify that the hazards will not occur and to find any hazards that may occur.

This chapter will illustrate the software fault tree analysis for the software portion of a system. The failure modes effects and criticality analysis (FMECA) will also be shown for a system.

11.1 FAULT-TREE ANALYSIS

There are five steps for performing a software fault tree analysis:

1. Determine the potential hazards of the software. These hazards may be identified based on experience by field or maintenance personnel or by a worst-case scenario. Hazards may be identified that have been known to exist on previous products of similar nature and/or that may occur based on the application. Some of the possible hazardous events may be:
   a. Failure of the software to perform some required function.
   b. Software performs a function that is not required and not desired or expected.
   c. A wrong response is generated for a hazardous condition.
   d. A condition that is hazardous is not recognized.
2. Assume that this hazard has already occurred and you want to determine the events that caused this hazard to occur.
3. Trace the software code from the top level down to some predefined level of design in order to determine what caused the event. You may have varying levels within the analysis, depending on the criticality of the hazard.
4. The root of the fault tree is the hazardous event.
5. The fault tree analysis may be performed preferably during the design phase and before coding is complete, in order to design the software to be tolerant to the defined hazards. Later the fault tree may be performed and used to identify test cases to verify that the defined potential hazards will not exist.
6. Use the software structure chart, hierarchy chart, and/or flow diagrams to do the analysis and also to determine the stopping point. The stopping point should be predetermined. For example, the stopping point may be the lowest module level. In this case, the fault tree would stop at the modules that do not call other modules. There is various nomenclature for the levels of software function. This author will use the following nomenclature for the fault-tree analysis examples:

- *Program Level*: The highest software level that would control all of the software functions.
- *Subprogram Level*: The next highest level that represents each of the major parts of the software. If our program were, for example, an operating system, the subprograms might be file operations, disk operations, utilities, etc.
- *Component Level*: This level is under the subprogram level and controls a major function of the software. Using our previous example, components of the file operations subprogram may be delete, copy, append, edit, etc.
- *Subcomponent Level*: This level is under the component and controls each of the compilable units that performs a function. Using the previous example, the subcomponents of the delete component might be file I/O, delete processing, etc.
- *Module or Unit Level*: This level is the lowest level of compilable units. Using the operating system example, the modules might be the routines that open the file, close the file, etc.

A fault tree analysis is illustrated next on a software program that was developed to output two binary files, each of which must exist in a complete and noncorrupted form for success. Incorrect data in either of the two files may or may not cause a critical failure.

The software consists of one subprogram that organizes, verifies, computes, and assembles user-entered data. We call this subprogram assemble. This is one of two critical subprograms. The other critical subprogram is the data entry subprogram, which allows the user to enter the data and which stores the data to be used by assemble. We call this subprogram output.

The other subprograms are not critical: They perform functions that aid the user in entering data. Although the loss of these functions would make the user's life more difficult, and certainly would make the product less desirable to the end user, these functions are not critical for success. The fault tree examples here focus only on the subprograms create and assemble.

The entire hierarchy chart is shown for the program in Figure 11.1. Figure 11.2 illustrates the flow of control in each of the critical subprograms.

Nine top-level hazard modes were defined for this software system and six were determined to be critical. These hazards are as follows:

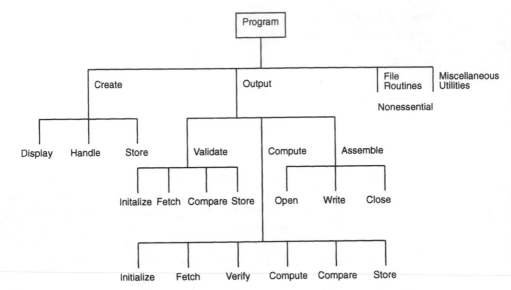

Figure 11.1   Software structure of fault tree analysis example.

1. File 1 not created at all—critical due to loss of data.
2. File 2 not created at all—critical due to loss of data.
3. File 1 and file 2 not created—critical due to loss of data.
4. File 1 has incorrect values—may or may not be critical depending on mission and incorrect values.
5. File 2 has incorrect values—may or may not be critical depending on mission and incorrect values.
6. Files 1 and 2 have incorrect values—may or may not be critical depending on mission and incorrect values.
7. File 1 is corrupted—critical due to loss of data.
8. File 2 is corrupted—critical due to loss of data.
9. Files 1 and 2 have corrupt data—critical due to loss of data.

The flow diagrams, hierarchy chart, and knowledge of the software and the potential hazards of it were used to develop the fault trees shown in the examples. A sample of the nine complete fault trees is illustrated in Figures 11.3 through 11.6.

Figure 11.3 illustrates the fault tree for the event that file 2 has incorrect values. This event will be caused either by the create subprogram or

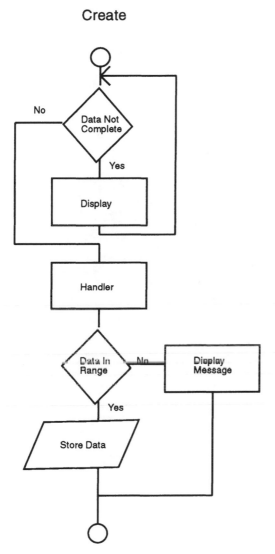

Create

Figure 11.2   Top-level flow of sample software.

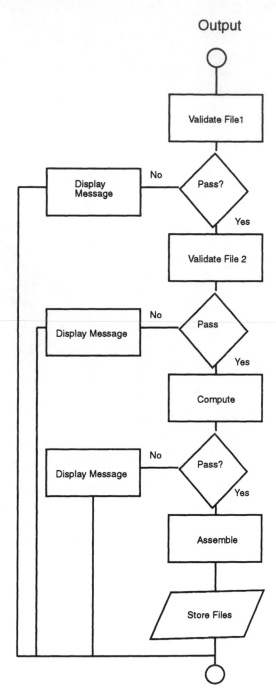

Figure 11.2 (Continued)

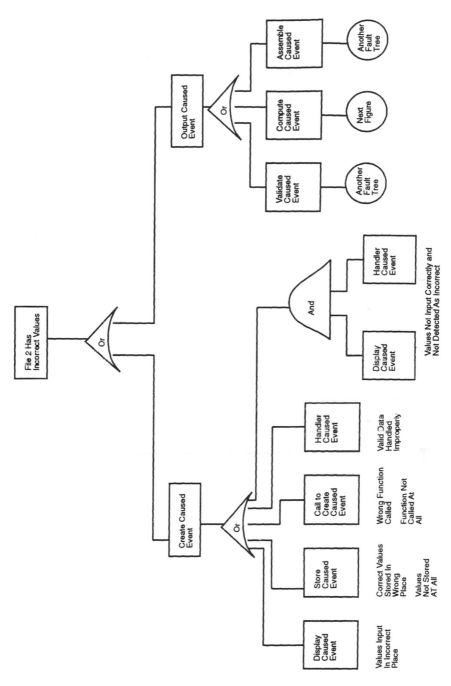

Figure 11.3 Fault tree analysis example I.

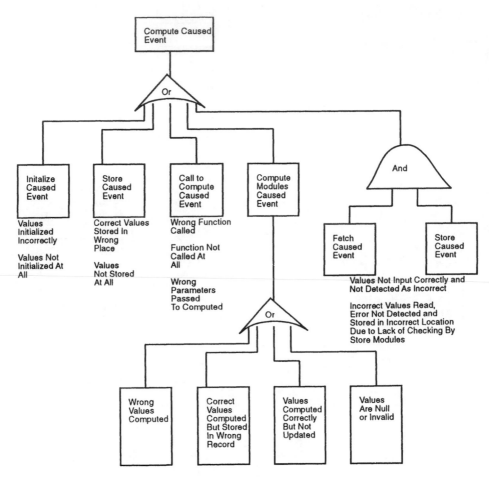

Figure 11.4   Fault tree analysis example II.

by the output subprogram. If the event is caused by create, it will be due either to the display, the store, the call to create, the handler, or a combination of the display and handler. If the output caused the event, it is due to either the validate, compute, or assemble components. The fault tree for the compute causing the event is shown in Figure 11.4.

If the compute component caused the event, then it is due to either the initialize, the store, the call to compute, the compute modules, or a combination of the fetch and the store. If the compute modules caused

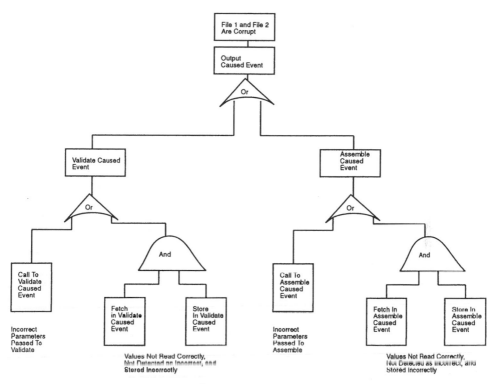

Figure 11.5 Fault tree analysis example III.

the event, then it is due to either the wrong values being computed, the correct values computed but stored in incorrect place, the correct values computed but not stored or updated, or the values computed being in-valid. The compute fault tree was shown, since the engineer knew that this component was historically the most common cause of this top level event.

Figure 11.5 illustrates the fault tree for the event when files 1 and 2 are corrupt. In this event, the corruption can only be due to the output subprogram. Either the validate or the assemble components must have caused the event. If the validate component causes the event, then it was due to either the call to validate, or a combination of a fetch and store in validate. If the assemble caused the event, it was due to either the call to assemble, or a combination of a fetch and store in assemble.

Figure 11.6 illustrates the event that file 1 is not created at all. Either

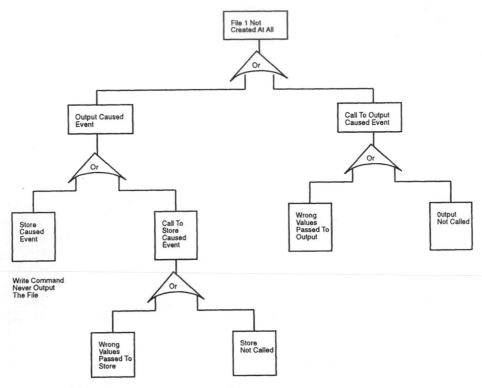

Figure 11.6   Fault tree analysis example IV.

the output caused the event or the call to the output subprogram caused
this event. If the output caused the event, then it was due to either the
store or the call to the store. If the call to the store caused the event, then
it was due to either wrong parameters being passed or the store not
being called when needed. If the call to output caused the event, then it
was due to either the incorrect values passed to output or the output not
being called when needed.

The fault trees were described previously as if the event had already
occurred. This is exactly how you would read them if you were creating
them.

The six critical hazards were analyzed first, and then the three hazards
that may or may not be critical were analyzed, to determine what incorrect values could cause a critical failure. The analyses for the critical haz-

ards were performed to the module level or the lowest level necessary to determine a potential hazard.

11.2 FAILURE MODES EFFECTS AND CRITICALITY ANALYSIS

Contrary to the fault tree analysis, the failure modes effects and criticality analysis (FMECA) is performed on software from the bottom up as opposed to from the top down.

The hazards are identified for the FMECA as they are for the fault tree analysis. These hazards are broken down to subhazards to the appropriate design level for which the FMECA is being performed on. For example, if the FMECA is performed at the component level of the software, then subhazards would be defined that pertain to the component level of software design.

Once the subhazards are defined, an FMECA is performed for each level of design (i.e., component) and for each subhazard. The system is analyzed from the bottom up on various levels of design. If the component was used, then the next level may be the subprogram, then system levels. The effect of the subhazard (failure mode) in question is analyzed at three levels of the system.

Finally, a criticality and a probably of occurrence is assigned. If it is known that the software has been designed to avoid this failure mode, then this should be reflected in the probability.

SUMMARY

The software fault tree analysis and failure modes effects and criticality analysis may be used at various phases of the software life cycle to:

1. Impact the design for safety and potential hazards.
2. Develop test cases to verify that potential hazards are not probable.

These analyses may be used in the design and coding phases in order to isolate areas of the software that may have to have special fault tolerances for identified hazards. They may then be used in the testing phase to verify that the identified hazards do not exist. The hazard testing described in Section 10.4 requires either the SFTA or FMECA analyses to define the test inputs.

REFERENCE

Levenson, N., and Stolzy, J. Software Fault Tree Analysis Applied to Ada, Stolzy, *IEEE Trans.*, 1984.

CHAPTER 12

Automating Software Reliability

This chapter discusses how software reliability models, software development, metrics, and analyses may be automated. Many of the models and metrics are cumbersome unless they are automated, and some development tasks are also cumbersome if not automated. There are few aspects of the software development process that have not been automated to date.

12.1 TOOLS FOR ESTIMATING SOFTWARE RELIABILITY

In the previous chapters we have discussed how to estimate or predict software reliability. Many of the models are not practical to implement in a real environment unless automated. Unfortunately, automating these models requires a variety of inputs that may or may not be easily automated.

Tools are currently available for estimating software reliability. Many of the authors discussed in Chapter 8 have automated their models. SMERFS was developed by Dr. Farr of the U.S. Navy and automates several reliability models. This author has automated various models into a tool that estimates software reliability and generates various trends and metrics.

An effective automated system should have not only the models automated, but also the means for collecting the inputs to the models automated. For most of the models the necessary inputs are the bug counts and time between bug occurrences. This information may be logged by a problem-reporting system or configuration-management system. An efficient reliability tool will automatically input this information and calculate the reliability estimates.

Each of the models requires slightly different inputs, which may or may not be available through automated mechanisms. For example, the models that require test coverage information will need to interface with whatever tools are available to calculate test coverage. Some information may have to be input into a software reliability tool by hand.

Each of the models discussed in Chapter 8 is reviewed in Table 8.2 from the perspective of automation. The inputs that are required are identified.

Ideally, a software reliability measurement tool will be able to not only estimate or predict reliability, but project those estimations, interpret trends, employ software metrics, and possibly analyze the software for fault trees and failure modes. Figure 12.1 illustrates a system such as this, showing the data flow of a software reliability tool that automates problem reporting and error tracking, product metrics, process metrics, fault tree analysis, and reliability trends.

Software metrics normally require detailed information about the software itself, such as the complexity per unit, errors per unit, maintenance actions per unit, serious errors per unit, maximum corrective action time, minimum corrective action time, and average corrective action time, as well as other information that is not necessarily related to error counts or time between errors detected.

Fault trees have not been known to be easy to automate, because they rely so heavily on human experience and knowledge. This author believes that an expert system with an extensive knowledge base is necessary to completely automate either the fault tree analysis or the FMECA for software.

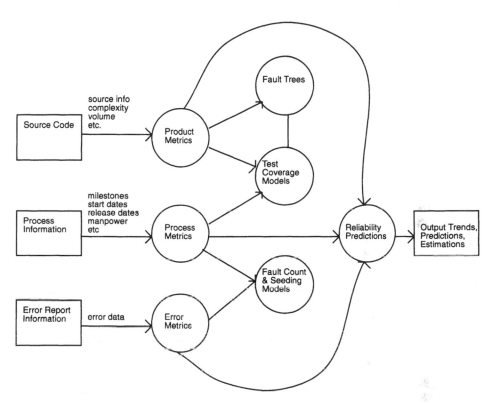

Figure 12.1 Automating software reliability.

12.2 ANALYSIS TOOLS

There are currently several methodologies for software requirements analysis. Most of these methodologies have been automated by various software companies. One commonly used and commonly automated analysis methodology is Yourdon's. The tools normally consist of a data flow diagram tool, a data dictionary tool, and a minispect tool. Some of the tools available today may generate a design (PDL) based on the analysis developed.

12.3   DESIGN TOOLS

The PDL generators may be purchased or developed by your organization. If you are considering development of a PDL generator, the following are guidelines for doing so.

1.   A PDL generator should be language sensitive, since the PDL will be contained in the actual source code. The PDL must be preceded by the appropriate comment delimiter for that language. You may develop the generator to recognize a variety of language comments and then make versions of it for each language. There are also some features in various languages, such as packages in Ada, that will be specific to that language.

2.   The PDL command will need to be distinguished from other commented lines. Therefore the comment delimiter will need to be distinguished so that it does not impede compilation but is different from the other comment statements.

3.   A PDL generator will use keywords that relate to the functionality of the real language commands. For example, "if" and "else" are keywords that relate to the generic branch in logic. The keyword "case" represents a multiple branch in logic. The keyword "dowhile" represents a loop that may or may not be executed even once. The keywords "repeat" and "until" represent a loop that must be executed at least once. The following are various keywords and their usage:

    if (some condition)
    else
    elseif
    endif
    case
    docase
    endcase

    for index (some range)
    endloop

    repeat
    until (some condition)

    dowhile (some condition)
    endwhile

initialize (some variable) to (some value) [Note: Use initialize when setting the variable for the first time, usually at the beginning of the source code where it is declared.]

set (some variable) to (some value) [Note: Use set when setting the variable to a value any other time after initialization.]

increment (some integer) by (some integer)
decrement (some integer) by (some integer) [Note: Increment and decrement are used normally to change indexes or counts.]

call (some function name)

return

end

4.   The keywords described in guideline 3 are the very basic keywords needed to represent branches in logic and commonly used commands. You may add other keywords to represent other commands.

5.   Now that the keywords are defined, you will need to develop code that will recognize the comment delimiter, read the keyword, and then organize the PDL according to structure. For example, if there were nested if conditions, the PDL generator should read those keywords sequentially and then determine which if statements belong to which endif and else statements.

If there is an error or an unclosed branch in logic, the PDL generator should provide an error message so that the designer may determine where the error is. The PDL generator processes in a similar manner to a compiler, except that it processes only a design description. A good PDL generator will also indent and number the branches in logic so that when the module is coded, the engineer will be able to easily identify the levels of nesting.

6.   The basic PDL generator described in guideline 5 may be further enhanced so that the actual conditions represented in the parentheses are recognized and interpreted later for development of test cases. The tradeoff in doing this is that the more sophisticated the PDL generator, the more cumbersome and time-consuming it may become. The reason is that the condition would have to be expressed by the developer in a very exact format and all designers would have to consistently express their PDL in that format. It may not lend itself to natural English description, which is useful during the later phases of testing and maintenance.

12.4   TOOLS THAT COMPUTE COMPLEXITY

Another feature of a PDL generator is the ability to automatically compute complexity. If the PDL tool is capability of identifying branches in logic, it should be able to compute structural complexity by adding one to the number of branches in logic. A PDL tool can insert the complexity within the source code, as well as indent and determine structure errors any time it is executed with the source code as its input.

12.5   TOOLS THAT PRODUCE TEST CASES

If a PDL generator exists, the means to generate structural test cases probably exists also. A test case generator that is based on structural test cases may be developed directly from a PDL tool. A very basic test case tool requires as inputs the branches in logic of the source code module. It also requires knowledge of the structure and order of those branches in logic. The test case generator will need as inputs the conditions for those branches in logic, also. Therefore, the PDL generator must be designed so that there is a standard format for the conditions that were represented in parentheses in Section 12.3. There mut be a standard format for relational operators such as $>$, $<$, $> =$, $< =$, and not equal to. There must also be a standard format for the logical operations such as AND and OR. Whatever that format is, it must be defined and consistent so that the test case generator will recognize it as a condition and generate a test case based on that condition. Some suggestions are:

.EQ.
.LT.
.LE.
.NE.
.GT.
.GE.
.AND.
.OR.

The condition itself should be contained inside of some delimiters also; (the condition) is one suggestion.

A test case tool may also output a logic flow diagram from the PDL to graphically show the test paths and test inputs. The test case generator will output the information if the keywords and conditions are provided completely and accurately by the design engineer.

As discussed in Section 9.2, adding these features to the PDL generator may allow for automatic test case generation, but it will also require that the PDL become more standardized and probably more cumbersome.

12.6 CONFIGURATION MANAGEMENT TOOLS

Various configuration management (CM) tools exist today that essentially keep a history of the changes on the source code. For medium- or large-size software systems, (and even for small systems), this tool is invaluable. Most CM tools keep a library of the versions of each module created. When the module is changed, only the changed portions will be stored to save space. When an engineer makes a change to the module, that person usually has to reserve the module so that no one else can change it at the same time. When the change is made, the engineer replaces it in the CM system and it becomes available to other engineers. These are just the basic features of a CM system; there are also many others.

SUMMARY

This chapter discussed tools for estimating and modeling software reliability, generating detailed design, generating complexity count, generating flow diagrams, and generating test cases for a given software system or module of software.

These tools were discussed because they have a very direct impact on software reliability. Tools that estimate software reliability and predict trends provide the development team with feedback on their process needed for improvement as well as scheduling. The tools discussed in Sections 12.3 through 12.5 aid in testing more effectively and efficiently. Without any doubt, effective testing has an impact on reliability and scheduling. The more efficient the testing, the more time that can be spent making the software more reliable. These tools also require that the software design be structured. Therefore the continued use of these tools may improve the software design.

The configuration management tool was discussed because source control problems may delay the schedule and cause software errors to occur simply due to incorrect versions of software modules being linked with other modules.

REFERENCE

Farr, William H. *Statistical Modeling and Estimation of Reliability Functions for Software (SMERFS) Library Access Guide*, NSWC TR 84-371, Naval Surface Warfare Center, Dahlgren, Va., 1984.

IV

Management of Software Reliability

Developing a Program Plan for Software Reliability

Now that we have discussed how to measure, analyze, predict, improve, automate, and design for software reliability, how can you implement it at your own company or organization? The task of introducing software reliability measurement and methodologies into an organization that previously had little or none is not an easy one. As a forewarning, the benefits of such a program are long term and therefore will take in many cases years to manifest themselves in terms of savings, cost cutting, safety, reliability improvement, and so on.

Unfortunately, software reliability improvement, as well as total quality management, is a process that is continual and ongoing. It does not end. There are no good quick fixes for improving software reliability, as there are no good quick fixes for improving any process. This chapter discusses the total process for improving software reliability.

13.1   STEPS FOR IMPLEMENTING SOFTWARE RELIABILITY AT YOUR ORGANIZATION

Before you implement the techniques discussed in the previous chapters for improving and measuring software reliability on a real development project, there are some steps that should be taken. These steps are designed to enlighten the organization about its own current practices and philosophies before attempting to change the organization to reflect software reliability methodologies. Do not be surprised to find that these steps take a year or longer to implement.

13.1.1   Research Current Policies at Your Organization

The very first thing you should do, assuming it has not been done already, is research what is currently being done with respect to software development and software reliability at your organization. You may find that you need to narrow the scope of your investigation initially if you work at a very large organization.

Determine what, if any, software development standards are used. Determine what, if any, internal software development standards are used. Survey the philosophy toward software reliability or quality. Some questions you might seek to answer are:

1. Are personnel at any or all levels aware of the need to develop reliable software?
2. Are any personnel knowledgeable to any degree about software reliability measurement or development techniques?
3. Have any personnel ever attempted to implement a software reliability program? If so, what happened?

This step is one of the first steps in any total quality management quality circle. It is part of identifying what problems in your organization need to be solved.

13.1.2   Research Current Software Development Processes at Your Organization

Determine, on a cross section of projects, how software is developed from concept to maintenance. Some questions you might answer are:

1. What development tools and methodologies are used for requirements analysis, top-level design, detailed design, coding, unit testing, system testing, and maintenance?
2. What tools are used for configuration management and version control?
3. How are the requirements defined, if at all?
4. How are the requirements translated, if at all?
5. How much effort is spent in each phase of the life cycle from requirements to maintenance?
6. How is the top-level design completed, if at all?
7. How is the detailed design completed, if at all?
8. What coding standards or techniques are used, if any?
9. How is unit testing performed, if at all?
10. How is the integration/system test performed, if at all?
11. Is there independent testing?
12. How is the software maintained?
13. When and how is the software retired?
14. How is the organization structured? Are there quality assurance, configuration management, reliability engineering, and systems engineering departments? If so, how are they structured with respect to software development, with each other and with the rest of the organization?
15. What metrics or models, if any, are used during the design process? At what phase or phases are any metrics or models used?

13.1.3   Research Current Software Development Practices External to Your Organization

Some current practices are contained in this book. There are many excellent sources for researching the software engineering process. This book contains an overview of some measurement, analysis, design, code, and test methodologies.

13.1.4   Research Current Software Measuring Techniques at Your Organization

Determine what, if any, software metrics are used, such as:

1. Errors detected by phase.
2. Errors generated by phase.

3. Errors corrected over time.
4. Errors detected over time.
5. Errors detected per location of source code or function.
6. Structural complexity per location of source code.
7. Functional complexity per location of source code.
8. Structural complexity versus errors.
9. Functional complexity versus errors.
10. Maximum corrective action time.
11. Minimum corrective action time.
12. Mean corrective time.
13. Rate of errors generated due solely to maintenance actions to errors corrected.
14. Other project and product-related metrics.

See Figures 7.14, 7.15, and 7.16 for a summary of these metrics.

Determine what, if any, software reliability models are used. Are any of the following used? If so, at what phase of the life cycle and to measure what unknown?

1. Musa basic or logarithmic.
2. Shooman.
3. Jelinski-Moranda.
4. Goel-Okumoto.
5. Schick-Wolverton.
6. Lloyd-Lipow.
7. Dual test group.
8. Test coverage.
9. Prediction models.
10. Other models.

See Table 8.1 for a summary of some of the reliability models.

13.1.5 Research Current Software Measurement Techniques External to Your Organization

Many of these metrics and models are contained in this book. However, there are many more that have been developed or are being developed at this writing.

13.1.6 Organize Data on Past or Current Programs

This type of data may be detailed information on projects that seemed to be successful with respect to quality and cost as well as projects that were not.

If it is available, collect information on:

1. Number of total errors found once released to customer.
2. Major source of errors (reason for them).
3. Estimated cost of maintenance.
4. Time spent in each phase from concept to maintenance.
5. Whether major milestones were met.
6. Whether software was delivered on time.
7. Whether the customer was satisfied with the product.
8. Whether the product was successful in the marketplace.
9. Whether the software ever had to undergo a major redesign.
10. Why the project seemed to be successful.
11. Why the project was not successful.
12. What development techniques were used during each phase.
13. Any of the metrics described in Chapter 7.

It is important to keep in mind one thing when performing this step. The success, or failure, of a project with respect to quality and/or cost should be described in terms of the process as a whole and not the individuals or groups of individuals. When determining the root of the success or failure of a project, determine how the process contributed to that end result.

In the case of unsuccessful projects, finger pointing should be replaced with objective hindsight on how the process could have been changed to result in a successful development project.

For example, the description "Programmers made many errors" is not a good reason for the failure of a project. It should be determined why the programmers made many errors. Was it due to changing requirements? new features being added? unorganized design, code and testing? insufficient design time? insufficient requirements translation from end user?

The average person may be included to look first at the productivity or effectiveness of only the programmers themselves. There have been many articles written recently concerning some direct relationship between "super" programmers—that is, those programmers who are well above average in developing code—and productivity and reliability. Unfortunately, the view that the more super programmers you have, the better the code, is an extremely narrow view as well as a viewpoint that is not conducive to total quality management.

The coding process is only 10–15% of the entire development life cycle. We have seen in previous chapters that many software errors are generated long before the coding phase. To assume that the coder or programmer is totally responsible for the reliability of the end product is erroneous. Without any doubt, there are various levels of productivity and effectiveness among programmers. However, this is true for any industry and any position.

A good development process utilizes the super programmers as well as the not-so-super programmers. In many cases, the author has found that even though super programmers may be able to write more code faster than many of their peers, they may also be responsible for costly maintenance errors and for hasty efforts in design and testing.

The total process is responsible for the quality and reliability of the software. There are many factors other than coding ability that must be investigated before you are able to improve your development process.

13.1.7 Develop Lessons Learned Listing

Some lessons learned are contained in this chapter. It is advisable to create a compilation of lessons learned for your organization and industry in addition. Keep these lessons learned stored where they are easily accessible to all development, quality assurance, and other engineers or employees.

13.1.8 Develop an Approach to Educating Employees

It is necessary to train software engineers, reliability engineers, and systems engineers in management of software reliability objectives and in the necessity for implementing a systematic approach to developing reliable software.

13.1.9 Develop an Approach to Integrating This System

Determine how you will integrate your system into the current organization. In the past, the author has been a software reliability engineer within the reliability engineering department, a software reliability engineer within software quality assurance, and a software reliability engineer within software development and has found that any one organization could not be completely responsible for software reliability. Though the reliability department may be able to measure or predict it, they cannot, for the most part, do what is necessary to improve it. Though the quality assurance department is usually in the position to monitor it and possibly collect data necessary for measurements, it also cannot directly improve it.

Tasks must be divided by every organization involved in order to impact reliability. Table 13.1 illustrates how each of the tasks may be divided among the entire organization.

13.1.10 Identify Particular Metrics and Models

There are some metrics and models that may be applicable to a particular development environment at your organization. A word of caution: Do not try to implement all models and metrics, particularly at once. Identify ones that, based on your past experience and knowledge of your process, may be useful for your organization.

If you have no real process for developing or measuring software, then choose the following metrics:

1. Distribution of types of corrective action (reason for software changes).
2. Errors detected over time.
3. Errors corrected over time.
4. Corrective action times.

Also, choose from Figure 8.14 a cross section of three models that are relatively easy to implement.

13.1.11   Automate

Automate to some extent the metrics and models so that the results may be interpreted in a realistic period of time; see Chapter 12 for some automation techniques.

13.1.12   Collect Results over Various Projects

Do not attempt to implement your newly defined software reliability process too quickly on too many projects at once. Choose a development project that is small to medium in size on which to implement your new procedures. Without much doubt you will have much to learn by your first project. It is better to refine your software reliability process before implementing it on a large scale.

It is also advisable to keep some of your plans from being complete public knowledge until you have had the opportunity to implement them once and refine them. In other words, you may find that you need to start a software reliability program from the bottom up as opposed to from the top down, with respect to your organization structure. Unfortunately, any time new procedures are implemented there is always the risk of increased cost. You may need a pilot program to determine how to keep these costs to a minimum.

13.2   IMPLEMENTING SOFTWARE RELIABILITY ON A PARTICULAR PROJECT

1. Develop an error tracking system that is specific to the software project. Tailor the generic error tracking system developed for the corporation.
2. Determine what tools will be used for (a) development (design, code, unit test, system test, maintenance), (b) configuration management, (c) reliability modeling, and (d) error tracking and data collection.
3. Determine which measurement techniques are applicable to the software being developed. Base this decision on both the assumptions of the measurement or model, the cost associated with the metric or model, and the availability of data for that metric or model.

4. Determine the responsibilities and organization structure with respect to software reliability for the particular project. Define who will be responsible for which tasks. Figure 13.1 illustrates many software reliability tasks and the entity who is primarily and usually responsible for them. Your organization may have a different structure, particularly if it is a small company. However, the tasks remain the same regardless of which entity is responsible for them.
5. If software is mission or safety critical, begin implementing the fault tree analysis at a predetermined level of design on the most critical portions of the software.

13.3 MEDIUM- AND LONG-TERM OBJECTIVES

Once your procedures have been implemented on at least one program, you will need to continue to refine them and broaden them.

13.3.1 Validate Models and Metrics

Once the models and metrics are chosen, you must validate them and continue to develop or research new models and metrics based on the results.

Once you have collected some historical software reliability data, you will be in a perfect position to validate other models and metrics that you have not used yet or are considering using on another project. By virtue of the fact that the data are historical, you know what the end result is of the software project corresponding to that data. You can input that data into some other existing models, assuming that the data are in a form that is usable by the model, and determine whether the model's predictions were accurate at various points in the development cycle. You may use these results to aid you in determining the validity of the many software reliability models available today, and to save time and money in implementing a model that is not valid.

It is not suggested that any model be completely discounted or invalidated based on the results of only one set of data. However, you should keep a running total from program to program of which models accurately predicted the reliability of the software at certain points in the life cycle and which ones did not. Do this for every program for which you

Table 13.1   Software Reliability Tasks and Responsibilities

Task	Primary Responsibility[a]
Research reliability estimation models	D, R
Research reliability prediction models	D, R
Select appropriate metrics for each phase	D, Q
Select appropriate models for each phase	D, R
Develop a problem-reporting process	D, Q
Refine the problem-reporting process for chosen metrics and models	D, Q
Collect historical data	D, R, Q, S
Collect error data	D, Q, R
Collect product data	D, Q
Collect process data	D, Q, R
Organize and analyze data	D, Q, R, S
Identify key problem areas based on metrics results	D, Q
Apply reliability estimation models	D, R
Apply reliability prediction models	D, R
Make improvements to data collection process	D, Q
Make improvements based on metrics results	D
Make improvements based on model results	D
Make refinements to models selection	D, R
Make refinements to metrics selection	D, R, Q
Manage problem reporting process	Q, D
Research software development procedures	D
Implement software development procedures	D, Q
Use structured analysis, design, code, test, and maintenance	D
Refine software development procedures	D
Maintain software development procedures	D, Q
Perform software fault trees and FMECAs	D, R, S
Make improvements based on FTA and FMECA results	D
Research requirements analysis techniques	S, D
Develop clear and complete requirements documents and specifications	S
Train employees on software reliability	D, Q, R, S
Maintain training	D, Q, R, S
Develop automated tools for each of the tasks	D, Q, R, S

collect data, until hopefully there is a cross section of projects with varying size, complexity, function, etc. At this point it may be obvious which models and metrics are the most accurate and practical.

13.3.2   Continue to Collect Historical Data

Continue with the task of organizing and evaluating historical data at your organization (if any) so that it may be used for prediction and purposes on newer programs.

At some point you may have enough historical data to utilize for predictive purposes. You may make predictions such as the inherent number of errors in the software, the reliability growth rate, the initial mean time to failure, or the initial failure rate.

13.3.3   Continue Evaluation of Design, Code, Test, and Maintenance Methodologies

Use the metrics and models chosen to evaluate the development process. If necessary, research new development techniques.

13.3.4   Continue to Refine System

You may need to modify who is responsible for what part of the measurement and development process. You may also need to add, modify, or delete tasks as necessary.

13.3.5   Continue to Automate the Measurement and Development Process

Develop an automated system that integrates the measurement techniques with the actual development environment.

13.3.6   Educate Employees on Process

Education may be implemented in the form of quality circles, as well as in formal education. Quality circles may choose to be responsible for:

1. Training new employees on software development and software reliability.

2. Training existing employees on software development and software reliability.
3. Tackling the source one software reliability issue at a time, educating the rest of the organization on their results, and implementing a solution to the issue.
4. Determining and prioritizing the current software reliability issues at hand.

13.3.7   Keep the Process Going

As discussed earlier, the process never stops. Though the improvement of the process will eventually stabilize, there is never a point at which there is no more work to be done to continue to improve the reliability of software. Quality and reliability efforts for software, as for any other product, are ongoing.

13.4   LESSONS LEARNED

The author has compiles a database of lessons learned from implementing, designing for, improving, measuring, and predicting software reliability. These lessons learned may save your organization some time and effort in setting up a system or program for software reliability.

Lessons Learned 1: Don't Expect Magic

If you are expecting software reliability metrics, models, and development procedures to work miracles, you are probably in for a disappointment. As many sources have shown, it may take years to fully reap the benefits of implementing procedures for improving the quality and reliability of software through a systematic process. A systematic process cannot appear overnight. Important steps in the process cannot be skipped.

Lessons Learned 2: Don't Rely on Only One Metric or Model

If you select one metric or one reliability model, you may find that the resulting measurement only tells one part of the story. You may even find that you have put your faith in a measurement that is not accurate at all for your particular set of data. You should implement various metrics to tell you various things about your process. Many software reliability models are based on assumptions that may or may not hold true for your environment. Don't put all of your eggs in one basket.

Lessons Learned 3: Don't Choose a Measurement That Isn't Practical

If you spend all of your resources collecting data for a model or metric, then you have defeated the purpose. You could have spent those resources making the software more reliable and using an assortment of measures that are not as costly but provide valuable information.

Lessons Learned 4: Don't Become Overautomated

There is such a thing as having too many automated tools and even too many standards. There should always be a place in your process for manual code inspections, other manual activities, and, above all, creativity.

Lessons Learned 5: Don't Implement Too Many Changes to Your Process at One Time

Implement new measurement and development procedures one at a time. Allow for adjustment time to each procedure before implementing a new one. You will be able to quantify the effect of each new procedure if you implement them in this manner. You are probably also less likely to fail miserably.

Lessons Learned 6: Remember That Software Reliability Modeling, Measuring, Predicting, and Engineering Is in Its Infancy Stage

Be aware that software engineering itself is a new concept with much to be learned. Keep current on technology concerning software engineering as well as software reliability.

Lessons Learned 7: Don't Attempt to Standardize Software Reliability in Exactly the Same Manner That Hardware Reliability Is Standardized

Even though hardware and software reliability are similar in many aspects, they differ in enough aspects that you should probably try not to mimic procedures you may have in place for measuring and improving hardware reliability.

Lessons Learned 8: The Objective May Not Always Be to Develop Software That Is 100% Reliable

In some circumstances, reliability is not an issue, or at least not a major one. (Such is the case with software that will be discarded shortly or is for demo purposes only.) If that is the case, then learn to optimize the design parameters that are an issue.

Lessons Learned 9: Don't Assign All of the Tasks for Measuring, Analyzing, Improving, and Managing Software Reliability to Only One Department

It is easy to think that all of the responsibility can be assigned to one group of individuals within the organization, such as quality assurance, reliability, development, etc. For a truly successful systematic process to develop, all departments must share in the responsibility and tasks. Some department may have the task of collecting error data, some department may be responsible for analyzing and predicting, and development is inevitably responsible for improvement and design considerations. The author suggests that a "software reliability" department is not created for the purpose of performing these tasks.

One approach is to have a software reliability function that consists of personnel from software development, reliability, quality assurance, and systems engineering. These persons would still report to their respective departments, but would functionally perform software reliability tasks.

SUMMARY

Many software reliability concepts have been presented in this book. This chapter described how those concepts may be implemented at your organization, and contained:

1. Steps for getting started.
2. Some short-, medium-, and long-term objectives.
3. Tasks and responsibilities necessary to achieve reliable software.
4. Lessons learned.

REFERENCE

Grady, R., and Caswell, D. *Software Metrics: Establishing a Company Wide Program*, Hewlett-Packard Company, Prentice-Hall, Englewood Cliffs, N.J., 1987.

Index

Analysis of software reliability,
  3, 5–6
Anomalies, 24–27

Basic model (Musa), 127–129

Code
  development of, 171–174
  documentation of, 175–177
Complexity
  functional, 48, 62, 173
  McCabe's, 173, 193–195

Data
  error, 114–117

[Data]
  historical, 96
  process, 117–118
  product, 118–123
Data collection, 81
  case studies of, 99–113
  error data, 81–94
  process data, 81, 94–98
  product data, 81, 98–99
Design
  conventions for structured,
    173–175
  objectives of structured, 171–
    173

Error correction validation, 92
Error prevention, 179

Errors, 21–23
  coding, 65
    data, 66
    initialization, 66
    performance, 66
    recurring, 65
    regenerated, 66
    undetected, 66
  criticality of, 67

Failure modes effects and criti-
    cality analysis (FMECA),
    213
Failure process, 30
Failures, 21–23, 30
Faults, 21–23
  distribution of, 74–75
    exponential, 74
    homogeneous, 75
    logarithmic, 75
    nonhomogeneous, 75
    Weibull, 74
  randomness of, 73
Fault tolerance, 59, 179–181
Fault tree analysis (SFTA), 204–
    212

Lessons learned, 236–238
Logarithmic method (Musa),
    129–130

Maintainability, 171
Maintenance action types, 85
  ambiguous requirement, 87
  anomaly not an error, 87
  anomaly not duplicated, 88
  change in hardware environ-
    ment, 87

[Maintenance action types]
  change in software environ-
    ment, 87
  documentation error, 88
  duplicate, 87
  hold, 88
  impractical to fix, 88
  inadequate design, 87
  incomplete design, 87
  logic, 87
  misinterpretation of require-
    ments, 86
  new feature, 88
  new requirements, 86
  performance, 87
  previous maintenance, 87
  requirements change, 86
Mean software repair time, 76
Mean software turnaround time,
    76, 95
Modularity, 171
MTTF, 75

NASA, 14, 39

Problem reporting process,
    82–94
Program Descriptive Language
    (PDL), 218–220

RADC, 33–36, 146–165
Redundancy, 182
  standby, 185
  voting, 183–185
Reliability models, 125
  case studies of, 147–165
  dual test group, 141–144

[Reliability models]
  Duane growth, 135
  error seeding, 140–141
  good ones, 126
  Goel–Okumoto, 133–134
  Jelinski–Moranda deutrophi-
    cation, 132–133
  Jelinski–Moranda geometric
    deutrophication, 134–
    135
  Leone test coverage, 136–140
  Lloyd–Lipow Jelinski–Mor-
    anda, 133
  Musa, 127–130
    basic, 127–129
    logarithmic, 129–130
    parameters of, 126–127
    predictive, 36–38, 146–165
    Schick–Wolverton, 135–146
    Shooman, 130–132
    testing success, 144
    Weibull, 144–146, 33–36
Reliability parameters, 75–77
Reusability, 59, 61, 177–179

Software Engineering Institute
    (SEI), 39
Software Engineering Labora-
    tory (SEL), 39–40
Software reliability,
  allocations, 40–41
  analysis of, 3, 5–6
  automation of, 215
    analyses, 217
    complexity, 220
    configuration management,
      221
    design, 218–219
    estimations, 215–216
    test case, 220

[Software reliability]
  components of, 3
  cost of unreliability, 14–19
  definitions, 10–11
  factors, 45
    documentation, 48–49
    environment, 51
    learning factor, 47–48
    maintenance, 57
    methodologies and tools,
      45–47
    organization, 48
    prototyping, 52–54
    qualitative characteristics,
      58–61
    requirements translation,
      54–55
    schedule, 57
    similar software, 58
    test methodology, 55–56
    tradeoffs of factors, 63
  government objectives of, 33
  importance of, 13–15
  improvement of, 3, 7
  management of, 8
  measurement of, 3–5
  program plan, 225–226

Testability, 171
Testing
  black box, 68
  configuration, 69
  life cycle, 68
    acceptance testing, 68
    integration testing, 68
    regression, 68
    unit testing, 68
  functional, 201
  load and performance, 69
  recovery, 69

[Testing]
  reliability, 69
    beta, 70
    data collection, 69
    system reliability demon-
      stration, 71
    testing time demonstration,
      71–73
    test inputs demonstration,
      71–73
  security, 69
  stress, 69
  structured,
    algorithm, 69, 195–199

[Testing]
    functional, 201
    logical, 199–200
    maintenance, 200–201
    regression, 200–201
  time,
    calendar, 96
    CPU, 95
    operation, 96
  white box, 68

Yourdon's analysis, 217